12-00

D1567564

Original
JOHN DEERE
Model A

Brian Rukes and Andy Kraushaar

MBI Publishing Company

Dedication

This book is dedicated to all of the people, both past and present, who have made the Model A John Deere tractor what it is today. The people of the past include the engineers who worked on this model, the dealerships that sold them, the farmers who operated them, and the mechanics who repaired them. Those of the present include the collectors, restorers, owners, and enthusiasts of the Model A. Without these people, the story of the A would not continue to flourish. To all of you, this book is for you!

First published in 2000 by MBI Publishing Company, 729 Prospect Avenue, PO Box 1, Osceola, WI 54020-0001 USA

MBI Publishing Company books are also available at discounts in bulk quantity for industrial or sales-promotional use. For details write to Special Sales Manager at Motorbooks International Wholesalers & Distributors, 729 Prospect Avenue, PO Box 1, Osceola, WI 54020-0001 USA.

Library of Congress Cataloging-in-Publication Data

Rukes, Brian.
    Original John Deere Model A / Brian Rukes &
Andy Kraushaar.
        p. cm.
    Includes index.
    ISBN 0-7603-0218-9 (hc. : alk. paper)
        1. John Deere tractors—History. I Kraushaar,
    Andy. II. Title.
    TL233.6.J64 R85   2000
    629.225'2—dc21   00-033238

On the front cover: In 1939, a revolution of sorts swept through most of John Deere tractor production. Many of the new tractors for that year were dubbed "styled," and the only row-crop tractor model that Deere left behind as an unstyled unit was the Model A's bigger brother, the Model G, The G had been introduced for the 1937 model year. By World War II, even the G had been stylized, although it had to be renamed the Model GM. This 1943 Model A is representative of all wartime John Deere row-crop tractors.

On the frontispiece: Collecting and properly restoring a Model A can be quite challenging because the tractors underwent vast changes throughout production. As a result, restorers cannot assume that parts from any two Model A tractors, no matter how similar the tractors may look from a distance, will be compatible with one another. Great care and research is evident in the quality of restoration seen on the nose of this unstyled 1937 Model AWH.

On the title page: One of the more unusual versions of the popular Model A is the ANH. Despite this version's relative rarity, it still conforms to the principles which the original Model A established—adjustable rear wheel tread, ability to burn inexpensive fuels, and amazing reliability. This 1938 Model ANH bears serial number 472957 and is in the collection of Walter, Bruce, and Jason Keller; Forest Junction, Wisconsin.

On the back cover: This striking collection of Model As, owned by Howard and Bonnie Miller, is representative of all five years during which the row-crop versions of the Model A were unstyled.

Edited by John Adams-Graf

Designed by Laura Henrichsen

Printed in China

Contents

Acknowledgments

There are many people who deserve thanks and recognition. Without their assistance and inspiration this book would not have been possible. I would like to thank my girlfriend, Rebecca, for standing by me while I was composing this book, as I know there were many when times that I was preoccupied with it. Also deserving of thanks for the same reason are my family and friends.

Much of the information and some of the photos contained in this book were gleaned from Deere & Company Archives in Moline, Illinois. Therefore, I extend an emphatic thank-you to the staff there, in particular to Les Stegh. Mr. Stegh was an absolute pleasure to work with, and he made sure that I had access to all of the resources that I needed to write this book. Without his assistance, the depth of information provided herein would be far less significant.

Finally, the authors want to express their gratitude to the following collectors who have allowed their tractors to be photographed and included in this work: Jim Joas; Walter, Bruce and Jason Keller; Don Kleven, Jr.; Lester, Kenny and Harland Layher; Howard and Bonnie Miller; Dale Olson; Lloyd Sheffler; Martha Stochl; Howard Ulrich; and Todd and Lisa Wani.

I also would like to thank all of the members of the Oklahoma 2-Cylinder Club, the organization that hosts "The National," perhaps the largest John Deere–only working show in the world, every year on the third wekend in July in Fairview, Oklahoma. I have been closely associated with that club and their tractor exposition for a number of years; without their support and encouragement I would not be where I am today. And finally, a special thank-you goes to Jim Cole for supplying a number of resources which aided me in my research.

Introduction

The John Deere Model A was a revolutionary tractor, and its record stands as one of the most interesting in all of John Deere history. This book outlines the history of the Model A and all its variations, describing the evolutions of the separate variations as in-depth as is possible within this book's limited space. Serial number guides, beautiful modern photography, and archival photographs from Deere & Company Archives provide further depth to the information provided. The author exhaustively researched a variety of important collections of primary sources for this book, the most notable of which was Deere & Company Archives in Moline, Illinois.

This book also addresses the very controversial topic of originality. There are no absolutes when it comes to this topic. Even though Deere & Company

did have guidelines when it came to decal placement and other specific details, not every decal was originally put in the "correct" location. Nor was every tractor immaculately painted. Additionally, customers could special order tractors with certain unique paint schemes, which further complicates matters. Nonetheless, despite all of these variables (and I have only mentioned a few), this book tries to outline what was considered "correct" at the time the tractors were assembled.

This is the second book in MBI Publishing Company's Original Tractor series. The first book, *Farmall Letter Series Tractors*, written by Guy Fay and photographed by Andy Kraushaar (who also took the photos for this book), covered all of the letter series tractor models in International Harvester's line. However, since this book only covers one of John Deere's models, this book can and will go into greater detail about that one model and its variations. The author feels a great deal of gratitude toward Mr. Fay for writing the initial work in this series, as it helped lay the groundwork for this book series.

How This Book is Arranged

Within this book, individual chapters are devoted to the specific style types of each basic model type in the Model A series. The row-crop models are discussed in the first chapters, with the standard-tread-type models discussed last. Each chapter gives an in-depth explanation of that model's variations, pointing out the differences from the other tractors in the A series. Also included is relevant information dealing with paint schemes, decal placement, and more.

The evolutionary history of the model variations is also provided, as this information is very important to a number of Deere collectors who want to ensure that their tractors are outfitted with the correct parts. Collectors also like to know when certain options became available and first appeared on these tractors, so that kind of information is also given. Unlike other books, this book lists the changes in chronological order, either by serial number or date, instead of by the components affected. This is done to give the reader a better understanding of the entire Model A at a certain time (rather than one isolated part of the whole tractor), since this is of utmost importance in determining if everything on your Model A is "correct."

In the appropriate chapters of this book, the issues of originality for each model variation of the A receive much attention. Usually, the normal rules regarding issues such as paint schemes and decal placement are given. Even though changes to this information appeared throughout the history of the A, these alterations are not discussed with the rest of the changes made to the tractors. Since paint and decal issues are the primary concern of many collectors, this information is listed separately toward the end of each chapter to make it easier for the reader to quickly refer to it. A number of captions that accompany photographs throughout the text also address these issues.

A Word About Originality

As stated earlier, originality is a very controversial issue. What is considered "normal" or "correct" for the average Model A may not be correct for your specific tractor. While there is usually no way to know *exactly* how a given tractor looked when it left the factory, tractors that still retain their original paint provide many guidelines on their own. If you are planning to restore a tractor that still has its original paint and decals, the best way for you to ensure that your tractor will be restored to as close to *its* original state as possible is to look the tractor over closely BEFORE you do ANYTHING else to it. Take plenty of pictures from numerous angles, and make and record a multitude of measurements. The latter will be particularly beneficial to you in ensuring that your decals go on in just the right location.

Also, always bear in mind that this is a hobby, and that means that it should be fun, no matter what. All participants in this hobby are to be respected, and collectors/owners have the right to restore or "fix up" their tractor in *any* way that they see fit. If you see a John Deere tractor at a show somewhere that has whitewall front tires, the wrong-sized rear tires, and is painted the wrong color (even if neon green or hot pink with purple accents), please respect the owner of that tractor and do not harshly criticize him or her for restoring their tractor "incorrectly."

Because of its subject matter and intent, this book does point out a few instances in which the decals or paint schemes of the tractors pictured herein are not "correct." In no instance, however, was the author intentionally harsh in pointing those things out, and much care was taken to be as respectful as possible to the owners of those tractors. Please consider any criticisms the author has made of those tractors purely as instructional, constructive criticism.

A Note from the Author

While I have spent much time and effort researching and usually triple-checking the information provided in this book, I do not claim to be an "expert" on the subject of originality of the John Deere Model A. I do acknowledge the fact that there still remain many questions about the A and its evolution, with some of the most significant remaining questions pertaining to originality issues. I am constantly researching these issues with regard to the Model A and other John Deere tractors, and new information is surely going to be uncovered with time. Furthermore, I acknowledge that some of the information in this book may not be correct, but at the time of this writing every item included in this book is as close to accurate as I could find it to be.

The row-crop version of the A retained the same basic appearance through five production years. The highly successful unstyled A, produced from 1934 through 1938, set the stage for the future successes of the A series tractors.

Chapter 1

In Search of the Best All-Purpose Tractor

You are driving in the country one day, and out of the corner of your eye you catch a glimpse of a rusty tractor nestled alongside a dilapidated barn. You immediately pull your pickup off into the ditch and park it, get out, and look more closely at the machine at rest. From the distance of about 30 yards, you can tell that the tractor is an unstyled John Deere, and you guess it to be an A or a G from its size. Desiring a better look, you jump back into your pickup and drive cautiously up the driveway of the abandoned farmstead that this tractor calls home.

You're there, right beside the tractor, and you realize that it is an unstyled A, and it is a 1934 model by serial number. The tractor is in sad shape—the front wheels are missing, the sheet metal is badly damaged, the block is busted, and the cylinder head and valve cover are lying in the dirt and weeds alongside the tractor. But all of those things do not matter to you, for this is an A. This is the model that refined row-crop tractor design, and you see a lot of potential in this first-year-of-production piece of history. You know a little about the A, but you want to learn more. Here is how the story began.

The John Deere Model A was the result of years of research and experimentation, and it was perhaps the most successful innovation in the search for the best all-purpose row-crop tractor design. Its tricycle design and adjustable rear tread width contributed greatly to making the Model A one of the greatest tractors in agricultural history.

From the beginning, Deere concerned itself with operator conveniences on the Model A. As seen here, the A afforded the operator a very wonderful, unobstructed forward view, which proved advantageous for almost all applications.

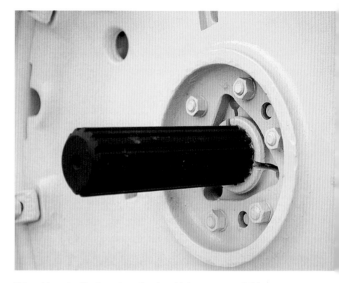

Wheel tread adjustment on the A, which was one of this model's biggest claims to fame, was made possible by splined rear axles. This feature remained basically the same throughout production, although the number of splines was changed along the way.

Even though steel wheels were standard equipment on all unstyled Model A row-crops, rubber tires were almost always an option. However, when considering styling changes for the 1939 model year, Deere recognized that there had been an increase in customer demand for rubber tires. Thus, rubber tires became standard equipment on the styled As, but steel wheels were maintained as an option.

Up until the 1920s, most tractor manufacturers produced tractors that were of a standard-tread design, thus limiting the usability of the units. Those tractors were sufficient for plowing, discing, harrowing, and other related tillage operations; performing belt work; pulling combines, binders, and the like; and for a variety of other odd jobs. Indeed, the John Deere Model D—which Deere introduced in 1923—was of the standard-tread design. The D and its predecessors—the Waterloo Boy Models R and N—had established the company in the tractor market, but that market was ever changing.

By the 1920s, tractor manufacturers had began responding to farmers' needs for a general-purpose row-crop tractor. The popular standard-tread tractors had worked fine for a number of jobs, but they simply weren't sufficient for the cultivation of row crops, so those activities were often done with animal power. Instead of just making "wiggle-tail" cultivators, horse-drawn planters, and the like, though, many farm equipment manufacturers wanted to tap the row-crop market even further by replacing horses and mules—the traditional powerhouses on farms—with iron. That mission catapulted a few former implement manufacturers into full-line farm equipment companies.

There were many different design ideas which companies made into realities in the quest for the ideal row-crop design. Some designs—such as the Moline Plow Company Universal, the

Allis-Chalmers Model 6-12, the Indiana All-'Round tractor, and others—were actually early articulated-type tractors, with the engine being mounted up front between the front drive wheels. Those tractors placed the operator in a position right above or beside the implement being used, thus making them compatible with (and in some cases exclusively designed for use with) horse-drawn implements. There were a variety of problems with these kinds of tractors, however, including poor maneuverability.

Another early row-crop design became evident in tractors that were called "motor cultivators." They typically had the conventional two rear drive wheels, but only one (though sometimes two) front wheel(s) located toward the center of the tractor's front end. Companies that made motor cultivators included Avery, Bailor, J. I. Case, Emerson-Brantingham, International Harvester, Toro, and others. The problem with the motor cultivators was that many of them were designed to be *just* cultivator tractors and were lightly built, making them all but useless for many other farm operations.

Nevertheless, the tractor industry had been somewhat successful in achieving the primary goal: to build a tractor that could perform row-crop work. More important, however, is that the producing companies recognized the limitations of those earliest row-crop-type designs. As a result, many companies were no longer content with having a tractor that could do *just* row-crop work, which all but required a farmer to own a standard-tread tractor for the other farm chores, as well. Thus, those companies revised their goal to designing a truly universal, all-purpose tractor—one tractor that could do all the work on a farm, including cultivating row crops.

The tricycle-type front end, which featured narrow-set front wheels instead of the wide, non-adjustable front axle of most standard-tread tractors, was one of the earliest defining characteristics of all-purpose row-crop-type tractors. There were a few often overlooked tractors featuring that design, including the Wallis Cub Junior 13-25, the Wallis 15-30, and the Stroud "All-In-One" 18-30. Those tractors were available as early as 1918, 1919, and 1921, respectively. But by far the most popular, successful, and well known of the early, all-purpose, row-crop tractors was International Harvester's Farmall (subsequently called the Farmall Regular), which was out by 1924.

With all of the interest in all-purpose tractors, it's no surprise that Deere & Company started looking toward that market, as well. Even though

Deere's Model AN, a derivative of the popular A, had the distinct advantage of having only one front wheel. This feature made cultivation of narrowly spaced row-crops possible, and it also meant that only three wheels (instead of four) were in contact with the ground. The AN used a front yoke instead of the normal pedestal found on most row-crop As.

Based on the Model AN, the Model ANH, which Deere designed for use in taller vegetable crops and the like, had more clearance than did the AN. The ANH also boasted a wider rear tread adjustment range, which was made possible in part by reversible offset center rear wheels.

Models AW and AWH look very similar, though the AWH features different, taller rear wheels and front axle knees that gave 3 inches additional clearance under the front end. Both models had the advantage of being able to have wheels running between two sets of rows, whereas the regular A, AN, and ANH had to run with their wheels between three sets of rows.

Deere's standard-tread Model D, which started production in 1923, had put the company firmly in the tractor market, Deere knew that it had to produce a row-crop tractor in order to flourish, and Deere wanted to have the best row-crop tractor possible.

Deere's attempts with all-purpose row-crop designs began as early as 1925. The initial experimental tractors were referred to as "All Crops," and they soon developed into the Model C of 1928. The C was a short-lived tractor, with its total production of slightly fewer than 100 units taking place in about one month. The Model C designation was then replaced with the Model GP designation, "GP" standing for "General Purpose."

The GP wasn't an astounding success, and even though it was an attempted row-crop tractor, it has since been dubbed the GP Standard. Deere recognized that the GP was not a successful row-crop tractor, so the company reacted by producing the Model GP Tricycle in 1929. It was the first tricycle-type row-crop tractor Deere produced. Deere soon replaced it with the Model GP Wide

Far surpassing Models ANH and AWH in ground clearance, Model AH was a true Hi-Crop tractor. It provided an amazing 32 inches of clearance under its rear axle, and it was so drastically different from the typical row-crop As that Deere had to design special implements specifically for use on it and other hi-crop tractors in Deere's line.

Model AR was the first tractor in the A series that did not feature adjustable rear tread. This standard-tread tractor served principally as a plow tractor, though many were also used extensively to power belt-driven implements such as ensilage choppers and threshing machines.

Model AI came standard painted yellow with black lettering, and it was also available with a wide array of wheels and tire equipment. The AI had a number of features that distinguished it from the basic AR, and all of those items made this tractor better suited for heavy work in close quarters.

The only tractor in the A series that started production, ceased production for a few years, then commenced production again was the unstyled AO. These well-designed orchard tractors were supplanted for a few years by the sleek AO Streamlined tractors, but changes in the basic A made it necessary to return to the original design style of the basic AO.

Tread (GP-WT), which was better suited for row-crop applications than was the GP Standard—but Deere still wasn't satisfied.

One of the main problems with the GP-WTs was the drawbar placement. Even though the tractor featured the row-crop-type narrow front end and drop boxes providing additional crop clearance under the rear axles, the drawbar was located fairly close to the ground and ran the full width of the tractor. Thus, the drawbar itself knocked down crops in some instances—a major drawback. This was not unique to the GP-WT, however, as International had already experienced the same problem with its Farmall Regular, and would also experience this problem with the F-20 and F-30. Minneapolis-Moline also had this crop-damaging problem with its Universal MT.

By the early 1930s, Deere & Company had even more reasons to not be satisfied with its position in the row-crop tractor market. The main reason was that most of its competition was catching on to the row-crop idea as well, and they were responding to it with some pretty good designs. To begin with, Minneapolis-Moline (M-M) gave the row-crop tractor industry a one-two punch beginning with its Kombination Tractor (KT) in 1929, which M-M designed for use with

Model AO-S (or AO Streamlined) was Deere's earliest "styled" production tractor. This tractor was vastly different from the Model AO that it briefly replaced; thus many parts cannot be interchanged between the more common AO and the quite rare AOS.

Deere was slow in styling the standard-tread versions of the Model A; the industrial AI ceased production before the stylization of the AO and AR occurred. The styled AR and AO looked and, indeed, were bigger and more powerful than their unstyled predecessors.

Though the A began as an unstyled tractor, Henry Dreyfuss and Associates of New York went to work to stylize the A and other tractors in Deere's line in the late 1930s. The new styled tractors featured slatted grilles and sleek hoods among other things, but Deere left items such as steel wheels on the options list for these modernized tractors.

Production of the styled Model A is often separated into two major periods. The first tractors, produced from 1939 to early 1947, retained the pan seat and other features of the earlier unstyled tractors. The tractors in the second portion of styled production, which ran from 1947 to 1952, featured a battery box seat, improved engines, and a different frame.

all crops. The following year, in 1930, M-M's Universal MT came on the scene. That same year, Oliver Hart-Parr's Model 18-27 Row-Crop, a single-front-wheeled, tricycle-type tractor was introduced. International Harvester (I-H) wasn't standing still, either; it introduced its F-30 in 1931, followed by the F-20 in 1932. I-H went into regular production of the even smaller F-12 in 1933. Other row-crops that were available by 1934 included the Allis-Chalmers Models UC and WC, the Case CC, Silver Kings, the Huber Modern Farmer, the Bradley General Purpose, and many more. With the competition having so many different row-crop-type tractors in their lines prior to 1934, Deere had to act quickly or suffer the consequences.

And act Deere & Company did. Deere started experimenting with a new design for a row-crop tractor in 1931; the first experimental units were designated Model FX. The FX led to the experimental Model GX of 1932. Deere performed extensive tests on the GX, trying out a number of different ideas. After additional improvements to the chassis design, cooling system, hydraulics, and even steering components were made, Deere authorized and began production of its Model AA experimental tractors, which led to the production of the row-crop Model A in 1934.

The styled AR and AO probably underwent fewer changes than any other basic derivative of the Model A, but the changes these tractors experienced were still extensive. This late-model AR, serial number 282104, for instance, has an entirely different main case and frame (among other things) than did the original ARs.

The unstyled Model A and all of its derivatives are extremely popular with collectors today, but these tractors are among the most challenging to restore correctly. After all, in only five years of production, these tractors underwent many changes, precluding the enthusiast from assembling a definitive collection of variations.

The styled A came along at a perfect time, coinciding with the introduction of numerous stylized tractors by a variety of manufacturers. Though current in surface appearance, some of these tractors were produced on the more archaic-looking steel wheels because of the increased demand for rubber in the production of items used during World War II.

Yes, the seat on this tractor is yellow when it should be green, but if the owner likes it that way, then that seat is fine being yellow. Restoration is a journey for the restorer, and everyone is entitled to "restore" their tractor as they see fit. After all, it's much better to see an "incorrect" A sitting at a show rather than see it getting cut up for scrap.

Whether being photographed for a book or displayed at a show, most tractors are well taken care of by their owners. Owners take pride in showing off the restorations they spent much time and money on, and it is always nice to quickly compliment people on their hard work and dedication.

The Model A was a tremendous machine. With the Model A, Deere had succeeded in its mission to find arguably the best row-crop design. The A was widely accepted and enjoyed one of the longest-lasting productions of any John Deere tractor with production spanning 1934 to 1953, and for good reasons. One of the main reasons for the A's success was that it was able to take on a number of different forms to suit different needs. The most popular of the As was the basic row-crop tractor with two narrow-set front wheels. Simply designated as the Model A, its production lasted into the 1952 model year, accounting for the bulk of A series tractor production. Despite the versatility and success of the Model A as an all-purpose tractor, Deere soon saw the need for more-specialized variations of the Model A. Not surprisingly, a number of the derivatives of the Model A also followed the row-crop design, the first two of which appeared during the 1935 model year. The first was the Model AW, featuring an adjustable wide front axle. The second was the Model AN, with a single front wheel. Then, in 1937, Deere & Company introduced high-clearance derivatives of Models AW and AN: Models AWH and ANH. Finally, in 1950, the last major variation of the A appeared: the Model A Hi-Crop.

The Model A was also available in a standard-tread configuration. The first basic model was the

Model AR (A Regular). Its production began with the 1936 model year, and these units featured a new serial number run beginning with number 250000. Also sharing that serial number run were the Models AO and AI, both of which also came out in the 1936 model year. The final standard-tread version of the A was the Model AO-S, or AO Streamlined, which Deere introduced in the 1937 model year.

Another important reason for the A's success was that it changed with the times at the right times. Indeed, basically all of the variations of the A underwent a number of changes from the time of their introduction until their production ceased. For instance, the A started out in 1934 as an unstyled two-plow tractor with a four-speed transmission. It featured a horizontal two-cylinder engine with a 5 1/2-inch x 6 1/2-inch bore and stroke, and it had a four-speed transmission. At the University of Nebraska tractor tests, the 1934 Model A produced 16.22 drawbar horsepower and 23.52 belt horsepower. At its final University of Nebraska test in 1947, the Model A tractor was styled and featured a six-speed transmission. With its increased engine size, made possible by a 1/4-inch increase in stroke length, the A produced 26.7 drawbar horsepower and 33.82 belt horsepower. But engine and transmission changes are just the tip of the iceberg when dealing with the Model A.

Another reason for the A's success was its reliability. Although there were occasional difficulties with the A, the series was known for giving reliable, rugged service in almost any conditions. Today there are still Model As earning a living on farms. Other As, after living a life of toil, are now receiving well-deserved rest, attention, and care in the hands of Deere collectors.

The "sunset" of Model A production occurred with the termination of Model AR production in the 1953 model year. However, the sun will never set on the story of the Model A as long as there are people in this world who are dedicated to keeping these tractors alive and well.

This Model A looks as if it is ready to be gassed up and get to work. Or perhaps it is ready to go "play" at a tractor show somewhere. The Model A is a perfect choice for a person who wants to do some light farming, participate in a tractor shows, enter in tractor games, or even participate in antique tractor pulls. After 40 years, the Model A is still as popular as it once was.

Unstyled Model A Row-Crops

Following the conclusion of tests with the experimental Model GX, things really started coming together for what would emerge as the Model A. On February 16, 1933, Deere published its Decision 4330, announcing that 10 preproduction row-crop tractors would be participating in field trials. Deere designated these preproduction tractors as Model AAs. Ultimately, the factory produced only 8, not 10 as intended.

These tractors were to have numerous design advantages over their predecessors, including a lower initial cost made possible by less costly materials and tractor weight reductions. The weight reductions also resulted in further advantages, including a greater horsepower-to-weight ratio and better efficiency. Coupled with adjustable-tread, larger-diameter rear wheels—making the tractor easier to roll while also increasing crop clearance—operating costs dropped even further. A final enticement emerged from the new valve-in-head engine that allowed John Deere to boast about the Model A's better fuel economy, further reducing operating expenses. The AA tractors featured a two-cylinder engine with a 5 1/4 x 6 1/2-inch bore and stroke. The rated engine speed was 975 rpm, at which the tractor would produce around 24 belt horsepower.

These new row-crop tractors were also easier on the operator. For instance, the reduced tractor weight resulted in better balance, making

This beautifully restored 1934 A has the original flat-spoke steering wheel with cast triangular-shaped hub. Additionally, this tractor is correct in not bearing the "MODEL A" stencil on the seat support channel, as that was not done until partway through the 1935 model year. Instead, this tractor should have the "MODEL A" stenciled on the back of the gasoline-starting tank.

Collecting and properly restoring a Model A can be quite challenging, as these tractors underwent vast changes throughout production. As a result, restorers cannot assume that parts from any two Model A series tractors, no matter how similar the tractors may look from a distance, will be compatible with one another. Also, even though the parts may fit and "work," they may not necessarily be "correct."

This is a Model AA, quickly distinguishable by the unusual air intake and the fanlike steering wheel. This tractor is an AA-1, identified by the barely visible overdrive shifter lever. Note that this tractor has the "JOHN DEERE" cast into the radiator top tank, plus it also has a "JOHN DEERE" stencil with the Leaping Deer, but it lacks the words "GENERAL PURPOSE" and the patent information. Also, note the decal on the crankcase breather and the unusual brakes and flywheel of this unit. Since this is an experimental tractor, its decal placement and style are justified by being different from production tractors. *John Deere Archives*

GPA472 CULT. 4-ROW W/ #69 GAUGE WHEEL & #94 SHIELD
DECISION 6306   SPEC. 6450   12/16/33

steering the tractor easier. Additionally, the elimination of the drop box rear axles and full-width drawbar helped simplify mounting implements. Finally, the tractor's new tapered fuel tank, more slender tractor frame, higher and further-forward seat position, and narrower radiator all significantly improved operator visibility.

There were two different versions of the AA; the primary difference was the type of transmission used. The Model AA-1 utilized a four-speed transmission, while the Model AA-3 used a three-speed transmission. There were a total of six AA-1s and two AA-3s built. Complying with Decision 4330, the first Model AA was serial number 410000, thus beginning the A's serial number run. The first AA, an AA-1, had a build date of April 8, 1933. Tractors 410001 and 410005 were the only AA-3s, meaning the rest of the AAs, including the last serial number, 410007,were AA-1s.

Initially, Deere thought that the optional three- or four-speed transmissions would improve the tractor's utility. However, Deere's Decision 4372 of July 31, 1933, announced that the three-speed AA-3 would be discontinued, concluding that the four-speed transmission of the AA-1 was superior to it.

Deere certainly learned other things from the AAs, too. This is evident in Decisions 4399 and 4400 from September 1933. The first announced a change from a 5 1/4-inch bore to a 5 1/2-inch bore, using five-ringed pistons instead of the previous four-ringed pistons. The A-61-R pistons were to increase in length from 7 inches to 7 1/2 inches. This decision also indicated changes to the pedestal, transmission case, and other minor details.

Decision 4400 announced that the Cuno Auto Kleen oil filter would be replaced with a Purolator filter. It also stated that the Vortox oil-wash air cleaner would be used on future tractors, eliminating the old bail-type air cleaner, which sported a bulge protruding from the tractor's hood. Additional changes included the adoption of a toolbox on the inside of the left front-end frame rail, and the implement-attaching bosses on the rear axles were to be raised in order to provide even greater rear axle crop clearance. The changes announced in these two decisions, which Deere believed necessary to warrant production beyond that which Decision 4330 had authorized, were to be made effective on January 2, 1934.

With Decision 4427, dated October 3, 1933, Deere decided to make a different serial number

TABLE 1		
Speeds for the Models AA-1 and AA-3 (in miles per hour as outlined in Decision 4330)		
Gear	AA-1	AA-3
First	2.29	2.29
Second	3.31	3.31
Third	4.69	4.31
Fourth	6.78	N.A.
Reverse	3.56	3.56

Shades of color are an important factor to a Deere collector. As is evident from this lineup of unstyled As, while two or more tractors may appear to have just that perfect shade of John Deere green when they are sitting alone, big differences can easily be seen when those tractors are set side by side.

plate to further distinguish the A from the Model GP. In size, the plates were identical, measuring 1 5/8 x 3 3/4 inches, and both plates were made of 24-gauge brass or aluminum. The new plate, A-578, featured different lettering and was to begin with serial number 410000 (a tractor that Deere had already produced). This Decision was to go into effect at the same time as Decision 4400 in January 1934.

According to Deere documents, a hydraulic power lift was to be available on the new A beginning on February 26, 1934, and could be used on all tractors starting with serial number 410000. The power lift was first installed in mid-April 1934, after the regular production had begun.

In March 1934, Deere & Company produced four preproduction Model As from serial numbers 410008 to 410011. Those tractors exhibited the changes announced in the previously discussed decisions. Deere later rebuilt the first three of those tractors into regular-production tractors. The last one, 410011, was supposedly scrapped on Halloween Day of 1934, but was later rebuilt into 412866.

Regular Production Begins

Regular production of the Model A began in the 1934 model year at serial number 410012. The first shipment of As occurred on April 7, 1934; the earliest serial-numbered tractor shipped that day was 410017.

It could be argued that, in the production Model A, Deere had found the best-possible row-crop design. From the start, Deere & Co. did an excellent job of pointing out the A's advantages in its advertising. Of course, Deere did point out the A's adjustable rear wheel tread

Steel wheels came as standard equipment on the unstyled Model A, and those wheels were originally painted completely in John Deere yellow.

The exposed front pedestal of the unstyled A is the easiest way to distinguish one from the later styled units. However, it is important to note that the front pedestal did not stay the same throughout unstyled A production.

This top view of a 1934 A shows the fuel tank with the filler neck centered up on the tank, below the steering rod, a location that made fueling the tractor a little difficult.

(from 56 to 80 inches), although the company didn't always promote the A's adjustable rear wheel tread as being its number one feature. In most cases, it was listed second. Many times, the first thing Deere mentioned in its advertising literature was that the A could burn distillate, fuel oil, furnace oil, and other low-cost fuels. From a historical standpoint, that advertising technique makes perfect sense though, because Deere had introduced the A on the heels of one of the worst years of the Great Depression—1933—and things weren't much better in 1934. Everyone was concerned about financial matters—especially farmers—since agriculture had been in a state of depression since shortly after World War I's conclusion in 1919. Deere knew that farmers desired low-cost

One can easily distinguish the preserial number 460000 front pedestals from the later tractors by their lack of the upper saddle support, which was similar to the one seen at the base of this 1934 model's pedestal. This tractor also has an appropriate radiator curtain and correctly colored lettering on the radiator top tank.

These factory photos of an open fan shaft A that has been in the field reveals the "JOHN DEERE" hood decal with the Leaping Deer and the words "REG. IN U.S. PAT. OFF" starting directly under the letter "s" in "Purpose." Also note the placement of the "MODEL A" decal on the back of the gasoline-starting tank (barely visible here) as well as the clutch cover decal, which, oddly enough, has been applied a bit crookedly. *John Deere Archives*

Originally, tractors equipped with rubber tires featured tires that had 45-degree lugs. However, such tires are now very hard to find, as tire companies now don't usually make tires with 45-degree tread for current farm tractor use. Thus, many owners resort to using tires with the modern lug angle, such as seen on this 1934 model, but it seems unreasonable to be too critical of this concession.

the operator a full view of the job at hand. Other selling points of the A that Deere promoted were its simple, easily accessible design, four forward speeds, and its centered hitch for plowing. The latter was important as it nearly eliminated side-draft, which was a common problem with many tractors.

Decision 4488, issued November 29, 1933, outlined what would be standard equipment for the general-purpose Model A tractor. Those items included JD-1213 front steel wheels, which had a 24-inch diameter, 4-inch face, and 12 5/8-inch round spokes. The JD-1214 rear drive wheels had a 50-inch diameter, 6-inch face, and 12 3/8 x 1 1/2-inch flat spokes. Additionally, 1 1/2-inch guide bands were to be provided for the front wheels, as were 4-inch spade lugs for the rear wheels.

The Changes Begin

It didn't take long after the start of the A's regular production before Deere started making changes to the model. While not all of the changes made to this model are discussed here, the major ones and many of the more interesting ones are. Most changes are listed in chronological order, either by serial number or effective dates of the decisions.

Throttle Rod

Only 10 tractors into regular production, Deere shortened the length of the speed control rod from 13 5/8 inches to 12 5/8 inches on A410022 in March 1934, as a result of Decision 6001.

Upper Water Pipe and Cylinder Block

Tractor 410190 was the first to receive an improved upper water pipe, which accommodated changes made to the cylinder block at that time.

Fuel Pipes

The fuel and gasoline pipes underwent minor modifications with A410859.

Steering Wheel

Originally, the Model AA experimental tractors used four-spoke steering wheels that somewhat resembled fans. By the start of regular A production, the four-spoke wheel had been replaced by one with three flat spokes and a heavy-looking center hub, which resembled a triangle with all three of its sides squished in. That steering wheel remained in use until early in 1935 model production, when a steering wheel with three flat spokes and a round center hub replaced it.

tractors, and burning low-cost fuels instead of gasoline was a big selling point for the A. Indeed, Deere put out a barrage of advertising literature devoted solely to pointing out the fuel efficiency of the unit, which supposedly provided farmers with a savings of one to two dollars per day.

There were a number of other Model A features that Deere did consistently point out from the beginning. Most of these features related to operator conveniences. For instance, Deere pointed out that one could steer the A quite easily, and the operator could either sit or stand at will. Deere also promoted the A as a lightweight, well-balanced tractor, which provided

A close-up view of this 1934 A reveals that it does not have a glossy paint job, and, indeed, it should not. Deere & Company originally built these tractors to work, and things such as paint distribution and decal placement didn't always happen exactly according to plan, thus the tractors were not necessarily "perfect" when they left the factory. The main concern was that they were mechanically sound.

Carburetor Throttle Rod

Decision 5673, published on July 30, 1935, stated that the A118 carburetor throttle rod on the Model A was to be shortened by 1/4 inch to 29 1/4 inches.

Toolbox

Supplanting the original AA348R toolbox at serial number 412518 was the new AA459R toolbox. The new toolbox was located on the inside of the right frame rail, while the original had been on the left frame rail.

Countershaft

Deere modified the A's countershaft at A412800.

Transmission Case Cover and Steering Shaft Support Assembly

Both of these items received alterations at serial number 413399. The original rear steering shaft support had the throttle lever located at the very top of it, while the newer support had the throttle lever located alongside the shaft, slightly below the top. The new support also made use of a new bushing and made necessary changes to the transmission case cover.

Fuel Tank and Hood

While the original fuel tanks had the filler neck oriented straight up, operators experienced problems with the steering shaft getting in the way when attempting to fuel their tractors with the use of a funnel. Thus, Deere shifted the filler neck of the gasoline-starting tank to the left a few degrees early in 1935 production. Shortly thereafter, at serial number 413879, Deere also moved the main fuel tank filler neck over about 2 1/2 inches to the left. This latter change necessitated a revised hood.

Drawbar Roller

A new drawbar roller appeared on tractor 414565.

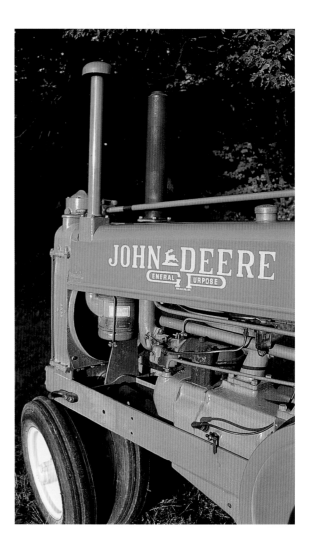

While many people think that only the 1934 Model As featured the "open" fan shaft, as seen on the left, the early 1935 models also have that feature. Beginning with tractor 414809, the fan shaft was enclosed, resulting in the style shown on the right. Note also the differences in the hood decals and stencils on these two tractors, both of which are correct as they appear.

Open Fan Shaft

All of the 1934 Model As, along with the early 1935 model tractors, are known collectively as "Open Fan Shaft As" because the rear portion of the fan shaft was exposed. Tractor 414809 was the first without the open fan shaft, as Deere had totally enclosed the fan shaft in a tube. Other changes made at this time included a new rear bearing housing, friction spring, and more.

PTO Driveshaft

The original PTO driveshaft included the gear and pinion; beginning with tractor 415082, the PTO driveshaft, the power shaft gear, and the pinion were all made separately, connected in part by a Woodruff key.

Governor Linkage and Controls

Changes in the dimensions of the governor arm and lever shaft first affected tractor 415709, with alterations also being made to the speed control rod.

Oil Filter Cap

A new oil filter valve cap appeared with serial number 416505.

Rear Axle Shafts

With Decision 5615 of July 1935, Deere replaced the A187 axle shafts with the A1091 shafts, which were 2 inches longer. This made the 56- to 72-inch rear wheel tread possible, without having to reverse the wheels. While this decision first went into effect on A423401, Table 2 indicates the earlier tractors that also used the longer A1091 axle shafts.

Manifold

Deere and its customers were experiencing problems with the flanges on the A36R manifold breaking, so Deere ordered (via Decision 5578) that the flange radius on those manifolds be increased from 7/16 inch to 1/2 inch. The first tractor affected by this was 420873.

Air Cleaner

The A's Vortox air cleaner underwent extensive modifications beginning with A422554, receiving a new body assembly and cup.

The First Major Variations Appear

The first major variation of the row-crop A was the Model AW (which Deere often denoted the "Model Aw"). This model was almost identical to the basic A, with the primary difference being the AW's adjustable wide-front axle. Available in the summer of 1935, this model was ideal for use on bedded crops.

By July of 1935, Deere & Company saw a need for a single-front-wheeled version of the A, which was particularly needed by vegetable growers, who planted crops in rows of 28 inches or less. This new model, which Deere designated the "Model An" (or, more popularly, the AN), used a new front pedestal and front-end assembly: a yoke. Deere used 9 x 10-inch front tires on this model. Decision 5640, dated July 27, 1935, estimated that 100 ANs would be needed for the first year of production. Since it was so close to the end of the production year, Deere built only

This tractor has the original-style, 45-degree lugged tires, and the "JOHN DEERE" lettering on its rear axle housings has been properly painted yellow.

TABLE 2
Tractors Fitted with
A1091 Rear Axle Shaft

421522 to 421537
421635 to 421679
421689 to 421695
421699 to 421700
421725 to 421810
421846 to 422289
422306 to 422308
422353 to 422356
422363 to 422365
422523
422525 to 422526
422528 to 422550
422653
422655 to 422677
423041 to 423285
423312 to 423348
423354
423389 to 423399

Sometime in the 1935 model year, the frame braces underneath the frame and in front of the main case were changed from being simply triangular in shape to the shape seen here on this late-1935 model, serial number 421367.

one AN in 1935, but over 150 would roll off the line the following year.

Big Changes for the Start of the 1936 Model Year Production

An amazing number of changes occurred to the unstyled Model A at the very beginning of the 1936 model year production, with serial number 424025.

Main Case

At this time, the A560R transmission main case, which the A had used since its introduction (which had in turn undergone a few changes, albeit minor), went by the wayside. Replacing it was the slightly heavier-built A1140R main case. One of the most important features of the new case was the new location provided for the oil pump in the bottom on the crankcase. This new main case also featured a different crankcase ventilator pipe.

Oil Pump and Related Items

The new B241R oil pump, located at the bottom of the crankcase, provided better oil circulation and proved more efficient than the original A25R pump.

Deere's new Model AW had the advantage of only having wheels in between two sets of rows, whereas the regular A had to have wheels between three sets. This feature of the AW made it ideal for use in bedded crops.

Occurring simultaneously were changes to the oil pressure gauge, oil pressure indicator, and other similar parts.

Countershaft

Deere improved the countershaft at this time; the part number changed from AA1593R to AA1153R. Accompanying the new shaft were new bearings and related components.

Brakes

At this point, the brake shaft and bushings, brake shaft pinion, and the brake housings were improved. Externally, one can identify the earlier brakes by having fewer holes in the end of the brake shaft than did the newer versions.

Main Bearing Housing

The A1146R left-hand main bearing housing took the place of the original A23R housing,

TABLE 3

List Prices
(Effective Nov. 1, 1935)

Tractors equipped with 24x4-inch front steel wheels and 50x6-inch rear steel wheels (or skeleton steel):

Model A	$756.00
Model AW	$800.00
Model AN	$756.00

Tractors equipped with 5.50x16-inch front tires and 9x36-inch rear tires:

Model A	$907.75
Model AW	$948.75

Tractors equipped with 9.00x10-inch front tires and 9x36-inch rear tires:

Model AN	$900.00

With its front axle sticking out in front of the tractor, the AW had a longer wheelbase and, thus, a wider turning radius than the regular A.

which had housed the oil pump.

Governor and Throttle Rod

Due to the changes made in the main case, Deere also redesigned the governor and the governor main case. Also new was a redesigned throttle rod.

Camshaft and Followers

Deere made changes to the camshaft and cam followers at this time, as well, as the cam was now responsible for powering the relocated oil pump.

Fan Shaft

A new fan shaft assembly, including a new rear fan bearing housing, appeared at this time. According to the parts books, the length of the fan shaft increased from 43 11/16 inches to 44 1/2 inches.

In terms of paint, the AW was pretty much identical to the traditional A row-crop. One difference, however, was the use of a "MODEL AW" stencil on the seat support channel (instead of the "MODEL A" stencil).

This 1937 A, serial number 459233, has the correct flat-spoke steering wheel with rounded cast center and appears to have the correct long brake latches. Later in the 1937 model year, beginning with tractor 464072, the brake latch supports on the unstyled As were moved forward, thus shorter brake latches were employed.

Magneto and Magneto Drive Flange

The Fairbanks-Morse Type RV2A magneto stopped being used at this point, and was replaced by the Fairbanks-Morse Type RV2B magneto. This change required alterations to the magneto drive flange.

Heat Indicator

On November 21, 1935, Deere began installing Stewart-Warner Corporation heat indicators on the Model A beginning with A 424851 according to Deere's Decision 5878 of October 29, 1935, and accompanying documents.

Toolbox Bottom

Beginning with all As made on December 2, 1935, the toolbox bottom (A494) was altered from

A number of collectors detect crooked air intake and exhaust stacks on their As, particularly the unstyled As. Ideally, the stacks should both be straight up and down and not look crooked when viewed from any angle.

it original design according to Decision 5653. The specifics of the changes are unknown.

Carburetor

Deere changed carburetors on this model at serial number 425821. The new carburetor used a gray iron body; the original was orange.

Oil Filter

Tractor 426562 was the first affected by a minor change in the oil filter head and cover.

Air Cleaner (Experimental)

Deere issued its Decision 5929 on December 4, 1935, announcing that 200 As would be fitted

Among the most confusing parts of the unstyled A, in terms of originality, are the radiator sides. While the A52R sides were used on all of these tractors, the position, size, and arrangement of the cast-in letters on those sides changed often. Most of the earlier tractors have the "A52R" cast such that it is readable downhill on the right side and uphill on the left side. Those sides have appeared on tractors as late as serial number 447775. Later tractors, however, feature the casting numbers cast basically the opposite of how they appeared on the earlier tractors, and the letters were bigger. Additionally, the JD logo often appears "below" the casting number on those tractors, and sometimes the letters "A," "B," or even "C" appear "above" the casting number.

TABLE 4
Tractors Using the Experimental United Air Cleaner

427101 to 427207
427229 to 427300
427940 to 427959

with special experimental United air cleaners for field testing. This decision, which was to be made effective on December 26, did not go into effect until January 16, 1936, on tractor A427101. The Model As that received this special air cleaner are indicated in Table 4.

Rear Wheels

Resulting from Decision 6118, 10 x 36- and 11.25 x 36-inch rear tires were made optional on Models A, AN, and AW beginning on March 18, 1936.

Skeleton Steel Wheels

In order to reduce costs, Deere opted to replace the French & Hecht skeleton steel wheels (Deere number AA-378) with Deere's own wheel (Deere number AA-958) as outlined in Decision 6093. This decision was to be made effective on February 15, 1936, but Deere documents indicate that it was not regularly enforced until tractor 454557 in April 1937.

AW Front Axle Knee

Though specifics are unknown, changes were made to the front axle knee of the Model AW at serial number 432072.

Cam Followers and Tappet Rods

Parts books indicate changes made to the cam followers and the tappet rods with A435283.

Spud Lugs (Special Equipment)

Deere's Decision 6263 on April 18, 1936, granted the use of the A-1298 spud lug on all versions of the Model A as special equipment intended for use on golf courses.

Rear Wheels

Prior to 1936, if an A came on the optional rubber tires, it was usually fitted with French & Hecht wheels. In Decision 5995 of January 1936,

though, Deere decided that it would produce its own cast-iron wheel centers for use with rubber tires, thus taking the place of the F&H wheels. Farmers could fit two wheel weights on each of these centers, one on either side of the wheel. Deere would also produce semi-drop-center demountable rims to fit those wheels, and the new rims would make demounting the newer tires with heavier sides a little easier. This decision went into effect on June 18, 1936, on tractor 438159.

Power Lift Improvements

Outlined in Deere's Decision 6275 of April 1936 were improvements to the Model A's power lift unit. Mentioned were the addition of a new control valve and an oil sump that was located below the level of pump intake port. Deere did the latter in order to help alleviate the problem of foreign material entering the pump body. One change to the power lift was an adjusted rate of speed at which implements were dropped. Other improvements meant that the operator would no longer need to hold down the pedal for any specific length of time in order to get the lift to activate, and allowed the rock shaft to return to the down position without any load (such as an implement) being present on the rock shaft. These changes went into effect on May 14, 1936, starting with power lift unit number P.L.-30000.

Spark Plug Covers and Cables

Published on April 25, 1936, Decision 6278 ordered changes to the spark plug covers and cable conduit tubes on the row-crop As. Deere documents report that this change went into effect on tractor 438177. With the changes to the cable covers, Deere found it necessary to alter the right-side spark plug cables on these tractors. Thus, Deere issued Decision 6380 in early July, indicating that the 22-inch-long AA-858 spark plug cab with safety nipple was to be supplanted by the 23-inch-long AA-829 cable. This was to be effective with Decision 6278, but Deere documents show that this did not occur until 438460.

Final Drives

According to the parts books, Deere made changes to the final drive gear at serial number 439353.

Oil Pump Components

At serial number 442151, the oil pump drive shaft was shortened and the top oil pump drive gear was changed.

Model ANH was affected by almost the very same rules of paint schemes and decal placements as were the regular A row-crops. Additionally, almost all the changes that Deere made to the regular A could also be made to the specialized versions of the A.

Deere's ANH offered a wide tread adjustment range from 56 to 104 inches. This ANH has its wheels set near its narrowest spacing. Many collectors prefer this spacing since it makes it easier to haul these special tractors.

TABLE 5
Tractors Using the AA945 Rim

460253	460970
460266	461034
460473	461068
460899	461075
460909	461076
460945	

Rear Wheels

Intended for use with the 10 x 36-inch and 11.25 x 36-inch oversized rear tires, the AA1434 French & Hecht rear wheels first saw use on tractor 442801 on November 14, 1936, by virtue of Decision 6724. These wheels were similar to the AA951 wheels with the exception of using type 8-T drop-center rims instead of the type 6-S rims.

Heat Indicator

Based on suggestions made by the Stewart-Warner Corporation, Deere issued Decision 6387 in mid-July 1936, which announced changes to the A's heat indicator. According to that decision, the number of the indicator was changed from EX-17837 to 92000, with alterations being made to the shaft pointer and frame mounting, all occurring at serial number 442897.

The standard front tire size of the Model ANH was 7.50x16 inches, while the standard front tire size for the AN was only 9.00x10 inches. This resulting difference raised the front end of the Model ANH by almost 4 inches. The true high clearance of the Model ANH, however, came from its larger 9 x 40-inch rear wheels.

TABLE 6 Tractors Affected by Decision 6687 of January 11, 1937	
454684	455150
454847	455151
454864	455155
454938	455158
454969	455159
455059	455160 to 455178
455081	455180
455083	455181
455092	455182
455098	455184 to 455190
455101	455192
455110	455194
455127	455196
455140	455197
455141	455200
455142	455202 to 455232
455143	455234
455147	

Seat

Decision 6506 of October 8, 1936, addressed the complaints of customers who disliked the tendency of the A's seat to collect water in a small puddle when it rained. Deere decided to add two 9/32-inch holes in line with the reinforcing washer of this seat in order to remedy this problem; this first occurred in December 1936.

Sand Lugs (Special Equipment)

On December 19, 1936, Deere's Decision 6646 announced the availability of AC-1029 sand lugs for use as special equipment on the A, AN, and AW.

Piston Pin

The piston pin went from being of the set screw type to the snap ring type with A445510.

Front Hubcap

According to Decision 6558, the changes made to the A1555R hubcap first affected A445325 on Christmas Eve Day 1936 and included a 3/16-inch deeper dish plus heightened bolting pads. This was available as special equipment on the row-crop As.

Rear Wheels

Deere's Decision 6752 and accompanying documents address changes made to the AA-945 and AA-1002 rear rims. The AA-945 demountable, drop-center rim, with driver and side ring, was to be altered with a gutterlike feature present in its base at the outer edge. The AA-1002 rim was to receive the same changes as the AA-945 with the addition of the rear side ring being

To obtain tread widths of between 80 and 104 inches with the Models ANH and AWH, the wheels had to be reversed on the axles such that the offset hubs faced the center of the tractor. With the hubs facing out as shown here, tread widths were limited to the range of 56 to 80 inches. These wheels are unique to the ANH and AWH, being standard equipment for those models. Thus, in order for the restoration of either of these tractors to be correct, one must not simply put on a set of regular A wheels.

replaced by a flanged base. The AA-1002 rim was first applied on A447102 on January 18, 1937, and was also fitted to A446973. The AA-945 rim first saw regular use on A461129 and was also used on the tractors indicated in Table 5.

PTO Powershaft Sliding Gear, Countershaft, and Idler Gear

While the first separately cast power shaft sliding gear, A1031R, featured 21 teeth, the new shaft, A1580R, which appeared on tractor 450504 featured only 19 teeth. Other items affected at this time were the countershaft with its idler gear, and the overdrive gear and shaft. Generally speaking, the number of teeth on almost all of these gears was reduced.

Transmission Overdrive

Deere provided a 1:1.71 overdrive on the Model A, beginning with 450504. Replacing the previous 1:2.06 overdrive, the new transmission provided about a 20 percent increase in drawbar pull and provided a speed that would satisfy a wider range of field activities according to Decision 6657, which instigated this change.

Radiator Shutters and Guard

Deere documents indicate that A450832 was the first to receive the new manually controlled radiator shutters with guard on March 4, 1937. Decision 6707, which first announced this change and was marked "A-RUSH," states that the new shutters were produced by the Pines Winterfront Company and were to be furnished as regular equipment on the Model A.

Radiator Core

The Modine Hy-Flow radiator core supplanted the Modine Turbo Tube core in March 1937 as a result of Decision 6776. The new core had improved water flow characteristics.

Governor Case

The radius of the A-1170-R governor case increased from 7/16 inch to 9/16 inch at serial number 454087 according to Decision 6877 and an accompanying document.

Toolbox Bottom

Decision 6687, dated January 11, 1937, affected one of the smallest things found on the A, but it was a large, far-reaching decision nevertheless. It stated that the A494 toolbox bottom would again be changed, this time from "Double Crimped, Intercrimped One Way, Square Weave,

This photo shows the evident differences between the Model AWH (on left) and the Model AW (on right). The AWH used longer front spindles in addition to the taller rear wheels. Both of these 1937 model tractors should be almost identical in terms of decal placement, with the exception of the model designation stencils on the seat support channels.

Steel Wire Cloth" to "Flattened Expanded Metal" in order to reduce cost. An accompanying Deere document states that this decision, which was to be made effective on May 1, 1937, went into full effect at serial number 455236 on April 27, 1937. The earlier serial-numbered tractors that also received this new toolbox bottom are indicated on Table 6.

Seat

Deere announced in its Decision 6970 that, as of May 12, 1937, the supplier of the Model A's seat would be changed from the U.S. Pressed Steel Company (which supplied its Model 1391 seat) to the Ingersoll Company (which supplied its Model PX-3109 seat). The new seat was not as flat in design as was the original seat; instead, it featured a higher back, which probably made operating the tractor for long hours less fatiguing.

Changes Made at Serial Number 460000

Sweeping changes were made to the Model A at this time. These changes are quickly noticeable from the outside as many were made for cosmetic reasons. However, some of the changes were made to improve the operation of the unit, and most of the changes were therefore well received by customers.

Rear Axle Housings and Rear Axles

Model A serial number 460000 premiered the use of the new A1866R rear axle housings (which replaced the previous A-828-R housings) on Models A, AN, and AW. The changes in the new housing were listed in Decision 6964, dated May 1, 1937, and included the raising of the implement attaching pads from 3 1/2 inches to 3 13/16 inches in front and from 3 1/2 inches to 4 1/8 inches in back. These changes brought the measurements within 1/8 inch of the dimensions used on the Model G. Additional changes included widening the lower implement attaching pads, changing the placement and distance between the mounting holes, increasing the number of splines on the rear axle shafts, and using new rear axle bearings which had a smaller outer diameter but a larger width. Finally, the most noticeable change occurred to the "JOHN DEERE" lettering on the

Since they were introduced fairly late in the 1937 model year, all of the unstyled Model AWHs should have the new style seat, as seen on the tractor in the foreground. The earlier seat style is seen on the earlier 1937 model tractor, serial number 449085, in the background.

back of the housings. Deere downsized the letters in order to make them match the dimensions of the Model G's F-226-R rear axle housing letters.

Hubs on Wheels

All of the hubs on the A's wheels had to be altered to accommodate the increase in the number of splines from 10 to 12 on the rear axles shafts.

Belt Pulley Assembly

A new belt pulley, A1864R, appeared at this time. In a related decision, number 6953, of April 1937, Deere announced that the JD7639 Hyatt #209 roller bearing would be replaced by the JD7950 Hyatt #1209-TS roller bearing to increase bearing capacity and reduce cost.

Pedestal Saddle Support

The new A1933R pedestal replaced the original A489R pedestal at this point as well. According to Deere's Decision 6928, of April 19, 1937, one of the differences between the two was the addition of yet another saddle support about 22 1/8 inches above the already present support.

Rear Wheels (Special Equipment)

For the Model A row-crops starting with serial number 460000, Deere offered the JD1235 steel wheel, which had a narrow 5/8-inch width and 2 1/2-inch rim depth as special equipment. Deere's primary intention was to reduce soil build-up on the wheels in clay- or adobe-type soils. This wheel, the French & Hecht #A-358-WG-508B, was approved by Decision 7594 of March 1938 and first saw use on April 21, 1938.

Drawbar End

Decision 6853 of March 30, 1937, stated that the A-506 drawbar end "having a large forged eye" would be replaced by the similar A1821 drawbar end with a 13/16-inch drilled hole. This went into effect on A460000.

Mid-1937 Production Changes
Magneto

As indicated by John Deere parts books, the Wico-type magneto on the 1937 unstyled A was changed many times. Production that year began using the Fairbanks-Morse Type DRV2B,

The shutter control rod on the unstyled A row-crops was originally painted entirely John Deere green, even though it did cover part of the yellow stenciling on the hood sides.

which had been used since the start of 1936 production, but by serial number 462100, that magneto had been replaced by the Edison-Splitdorf Type CD unit. It was used on only 400 tractors before Deere went back to using the Fairbanks-Morse. Deere then used that magneto from serial numbers 462500 to 464499. Beginning with tractor 464500 through 465099, Deere used the Edison-Splitdorf Type CD. Again, the DRV2B replaced it, being used up to tractor 466399. Tractors 466400 and later all used the Edison-Splitdorf Type CD magneto.

Brake Latches

At serial number 464072, the brake latch mounts were moved forward 9/16-inch and shortened from 1 1/2 inch to 15/16 inches as a result of Decision 7075.

Radiator and Radiator Shutters

The number of rows of cores in the radiator was increased from two to three at A464229, the result of Decision 7279 of September 3, 1937. This

This unit features the optional power lift. Tractors that have neither that feature nor the PTO are said to be "flat tail" models, despite the fact that the cover for the rear end is curved.

Bearing serial number 470232, this 1937 AWH correctly features the upper saddle support. This tractor should also have the 12-spline rear axles with the rear axle housings featuring the smaller cast "JOHN DEERE" lettering, as well as all other changes and improvements that Deere made to the Model A at serial number 460000.

Use of the clutch pulley decal on these tractors is often sporadic, as not all tractors left the factory with them. However, the location of the decal on this tractor is appropriate.

TABLE 7

Speeds of
Models ANH and AWH
(in miles per hour as outlined in Decision 7253) of September 9, 1937

First	2.57
Second	3.37
Third	4.39
Fourth	5.76
Reverse	4.08

was done in order to prevent excess water consumption of tractors fitted with radiator curtains when operating under full load during hot summers.

The radiator shutters were almost totally redesigned with A471568. The alterations were also made to make the cooling system more efficient.

Two More Variations Appear

After the introduction of the new Models AN and AW in 1935, it was some time before Deere saw a need for any additional variations of its row-crop A series tractors. Late in 1937, however, Deere recognized a new demand and reacted accordingly.

On September 9, 1937, Deere & Company published Decision 7253, authorizing production of the new "Model Anh" (ANH). The tractor's purpose was to provide greater adaptability in vegetable crop use. This was done by placing

Extensions for the skeleton-type rear steel wheels on the unstyled A are quite rare. These were often used in sandy soils to provide better traction.

9 x 40-inch rear tires on the tractor—which boosted crop clearance 2 inches—and by narrowing the bottom of the rear axle housing where the drawbar attached. This also increased crop clearance in that isolated area. Instead of the 9 x 10-inch front tire previously used, the ANH featured a taller and narrower 7.5 x 16-inch tire. The taller tire provided an additional 3 3/4-inch clearance under the front end, but the narrower width (which increased clearance between crop rows) required a change in the width of the yoke; it was decreased from 14 1/2 inches to 13 3/4 inches. The rear axles of the ANH were also altered. The axle housings were lengthened 2 1/2 inches, and the total width of the rear axles was increased from 82 1/2 to 98 inches. This allowed for an increased tread adjustment range of 56 to 104 inches; the range of 80 to 104 inches was made possible by reversing the wheels (which had the rim offset 6 inches from the center of the hub). Steel wheels were not an option on this model, likely due to the increased speeds of the tractor as a result of the larger rear wheels.

On October 2, 1937, Deere's Decision 7254 announced the new "Model Awh" (AWH). In many respects, the differences between the AWH and the AW were similar to those differences between the ANH and the AN. The AWH featured the same rubber-tired rear wheels; rear axles, housings, and tread widths; and the same speeds of the ANH. However, the AWH had only 3 inches additional clearance under the front end than did the AW, made possible by using the front axle knees as used on the Model BWH and 5.50x16-inch front tires. The adjustable front axle came standard and was adjustable from 42 5/8 to 54 5/8 inches. However, special equipment for the AWH included two different front axle extensions. The 7-inch extensions (AB-1350) provided a front tread width of 56 5/8 to 66 5/8 inches, while the 13-inch extensions (AB-1351) provided a front tread width of 68 5/8 to 80 5/8 inches.

Both the ANH and the AWH began production in the 1938 model year, and—just like the AN and the AW—their serial numbers were interspersed with those of the regular A. With only 26 ANHs and 27 AWHs produced in 1938, these two models are among the rarest of the unstyled As.

Late Changes to the Unstyled A
Offset Front End (Special Equipment)

Decision 7530, which Deere issued on February 2, 1938, is one of the most interesting regarding the unstyled Model A. In response to

The cast-iron Kay Brunner wheels were not as heavily cast as the centers most often found on Deere's letter series tractors. To compensate for the resultant lack of strength, these optional Kay Brunner centers had reinforcing seams on the inside.

demand from the Portland Branch House, the decision indicated that Deere would produce a special front-end assembly that would make operation of the Model A smoother in corrugated, irrigated hayland. The result was something similar to the later, famous "Roll-O-Matic" front end, though it was less elaborate and probably less effective. Deere assigned part number AA-1705 to this special assembly, calling it an "offset knuckle assembly including spindle and dust cover." This assembly allowed for one front wheel to be placed 5 1/2 inches behind the other, making it necessary to spread the front wheels

Basically all of the hood decals on the unstyled Model As should be centered on the hood sides. However, some photos of the very early-1934 models show the hood decals to be located slightly higher than center.

Even if you restore your A and the purists say it isn't perfect, you should still be proud of your restoration. Some people even put special mounts or pads on their tractors, such as on the frame of this one, to avoid chipping the paint.

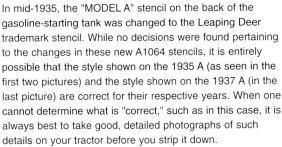

In mid-1935, the "MODEL A" stencil on the back of the gasoline-starting tank was changed to the Leaping Deer trademark stencil. While no decisions were found pertaining to the changes in these new A1064 stencils, it is entirely possible that the style shown on the 1935 A (as seen in the first two pictures) and the style shown on the 1937 A (in the last picture) are correct for their respective years. When one cannot determine what is "correct," such as in this case, it is always best to take good, detailed photographs of such details on your tractor before you strip it down.

about 1 9/16 inches. This arrangement undoubtedly made operation in irrigated lands smoother since front-end drop-offs would have been less severe, but this solution was likely not nearly as effective as the later Roll-O-Matic. Deere documents indicate that this decision went into effect on April 7, 1938.

Special Equipment for ANH and AWH

In order to expand the special-equipment lists for Models ANH and AWH, and to more closely match those lists for the related Models AN and AW, Deere issued Decision 7555 in February 1938. Items that were approved as special equipment for those high-clearance models are listed in Table 8.

As these pictures show, even something as simple as a drawbar can be different from previous years. Prior to serial number 460000 in the 1937 model year, the As sported a "loop" drawbar like the one seen on the 1936 A at left. Later models featured the more conventional drawbar end, as seen on the tractor at right. These photos also illustrate the effects of not totally disassembling parts (such as the drawbar assembly) before they are painted.

Cylinder Head

Although the cylinder head on the unstyled A appeared to be almost the same throughout production, there were a few changes to that engine component that are often overlooked. For instance, the A587R cylinder head found on tractor 475074 was the first to feature the increased exhaust valve port size (1 11/16 inch as opposed to 1 5/8 inch) and other minor internal changes outlined in Decision 7574 in February 1938.

Paint and Decals

Around the beginning of production for the Model A, Deere released a number of decisions that affected, in part, the "branding" or "stenciling" of these tractors. Because of the issue dates of these decisions and the dates they were supposed

to be made effective, it is often confusing as to exactly when certain things began.

For instance, the company's Decision 4763, dated June 5, 1934, concerns the "MODEL A" stencil on the gasoline starting tank of the tractor. The decision states that the letters of those words were to be 1 1/4 inches tall, and the total width of the stencil was to be 5 inches long. The letter "A" was to be centered below the word "MODEL" and these were to be silk stenciled (or silk screened) onto the gas tank with yellow paint in order to both distinguish the tractor's model and improve its appearance. The decision indicates that this was to go into effect on April 9, 1934, but accompanying Deere documents show that the first preproduction A—serial

No two cans of John Deere green are exactly alike. Thus, it is advisable to try to paint all of your pieces at the same time using the same can of thoroughly mixed paint. If you need more than one can, it is best to mix them together if possible.

number 410008—received this stencil on March 20 of that year.

Deere also issued Decision 4768, on June 5, 1934, which dealt with the stenciling of the Model A. It stated that the letter height of the hood stencil was to be reduced from 3 inches to 2 3/4 inches, and the space between the lines was to be reduced from 5/8 inch to 1/2 inch. Additionally, the words "REG. IN U.S. PAT. OFF." were to be moved from their centered location to the right, with the first letter starting directly under the letter "S" in the words "GENERAL PURPOSE." These changes were made principally to improve the appearance of the tractors.

This decision was to be made effective "Now," but it is entirely possible that it went into effect at the same time as Decision 4763. However, it is also possible that the first few As featured the original stencil with larger letters and centered patent office registration notice.

Hood and Model Designation Stencils

As a result of Decision 5440 of April 19, 1935, the hood stencil on the Model A changed starting on August 21, 1935, according to Deere documents. The words "REG. IN U.S. PAT. OFF." were centered under the large letters "G" and "P" of the words "GENERAL PURPOSE." Those

TABLE 8

Special Equipment Items Approved for Use on Models ANH and AWH

AA-471	Low air stacks
AA-511	Valve seat reamer
AA-533	Adjustable reamer
AA-640	Light assembly
AA-1098	Alemite hydraulic compressor
AA-1100	Power Lift
AA-1424	1:2.75 Overdrive
AA-1580	Fenders
A-1045	Wrench for rear axle nut
AD-345	Export tools

two letters (and, thus, the total width of those two words) extended for 15 7/16 inches total according to Deere documents, and they sported flatter tops and bottoms than were used on the earlier stencils. The total width of the "JOHN DEERE" lettering was to be 24 9/16 inches, with the letters being 2 1/2 inches tall although Decison 5440 stated that they were to be 3 inches tall. The "Leaping Deer" was eliminated from the hood stencil.

Decision 5440 also resulted in other stencil changes to the unstyled A at the same time. The designation stencil was moved to the seat support channel and was altered to read "MODEL – A" with 3/4-inch letters. The total stencil extended

for 5 13/16 inches, according to Deere documents. The new stencil for the back of the gasoline-starting tank read "JOHN DEERE" on the top in a curved format, while it read "MOLINE, ILL." on the bottom and in a straight line. Nestled between those two word groupings were the "Leaping Deer" (or "Deer jumping over the log"); its head stuck up between the words "JOHN" and "DEERE." This new stencil is known as the A1064 5 1/2-inch Leaping Deer Trademark stencil.

Patent Transfers

At the request of the Patent Department, the numbers "1,958,735" and "1,961,445" were to be added to the crankcase breather decalcomania transfers. This was outlined in Decision 5188, which was scheduled to first go in effect between January and March 1935.

Special Stenciling for Models AN and AW

Decision 5807 of late September 1935 addressed the placement of stencils on the newer versions of the Model A, including row-crop Models AN and AW. The decision indicated that these two models were to have the A-1063 stencil placed on both sides of the hood. Additionally, the AN would have the "MODEL AN" stencil placed on its seat support channel. Similarly, the AW would have the "MODEL AW" stencil on its seat support channel. These changes were to go in effect around November 1, 1935.

Branding Color

With Decision 6097, issued in January 25, 1936, Deere announced that the standard color for the branding of its products would be Yellow Color #2239. An accompanying document indicates that this went into effect on February 22, 1936.

The unstyled Model A is one of the most satisfying tractors to collect, and the contributions it made to the tractor industry will live on forever.

Chapter 3

The Early-Styled A Row-Crops

The story of the styled Model A does not begin in 1939 when those tractors were first introduced. The idea of styling had actually been around for years. At first, though, a number of companies—including Deere—dismissed the idea, stating that they felt sure farmers were more interested in functionality and not on how a tractor *looked*. Nevertheless, there were a few daring companies that took risks and, in the process, started a styling revolution.

One of the earliest successful styled tractors was indeed a green one, but it wasn't John Deere's. Rather, it was the Oliver Hart-Parr Model 70 of 1935. The styling on this tractor involved louvered engine side panels, a sleek frame, gently curving fenders, and even a hood ornament. Furthermore, the 70 had an impressive paint scheme that some felt gave it a soothing appearance while still making a bold, eye-catching statement. In 1935, nothing else on the

market looked anything like the 70—but that would soon change.

Minneapolis-Moline Power Implement Company was the next company to make a bold move in styling when it introduced the Model ZT in 1936. Sporting bold Prairie Gold paint with red trim, the ZT was nothing less than a fashion statement. Like Oliver's 70, M-M's bombshell also sported an enclosed sloping grill, but it boasted "teardrop"-style louvered engine side panels and M-M's revolutionary Vision-lined styling.

Up until 1937, Deere's tractors were still largely "unstyled." The beginning of styling for Deere, at least in a sense, began in 1937. That year, Deere came out with its AO Streamlined and, in the fall, approached Henry Dreyfuss with the idea of styling its tractors. Dreyfuss, an industrial designer in New York City, knew little about tractors, much less about John Deere. But to Dreyfuss, the idea of styling tractors was intriguing. Even more important, it was a challenge, and one that Dreyfuss was willing to accept.

The first models Dreyfuss concentrated on were the A and B. Less than a month after Deere first approached Dreyfuss, he presented a wooden mockup of the B. The project progressed quite quickly, and in June 1938, Deere published Decision 7750, initializing the plans to style the row-crop versions of the A. The project culminated on August 1, 1938, when the first 1939 model styled A rolled off the line.

In 1939, a revolution of sorts swept across almost all John Deere tractor production. Many of the new tractors for that year were dubbed "styled," and the only row-crop tractor model that Deere left behind as an unstyled unit was the Model A's bigger brother, the Model G, which had been introduced for the 1937 model year. By World War II, even the G had been stylized, although it had to be redesignated the Model GM. Thus, the look that this 1944 Model A sports is therefore representative of all wartime John Deere row-crop tractors.

From unstyled to styled, the A had already undergone vast alterations. But the changes made at the beginning of 1939 were far more noticeable than any changes that had come before. And the "Dreyfuss Touch" did much more than make the tractors more attractive—it also made them easier and safer to use.

Decision 7750 was a major undertaking for Deere, as is evident from its size alone. While most decisions took up a page or less, 7750 covered 35 pages. One sentence contained in that document beautifully outlines the entire purpose and process of stylization: "To improve appearance of Model A-An-Anh-Aw-Awh Tractors, we will adopt styling in simple lines calculated to bring out the impression of ruggedness and strength."

The new 1939 As looked strikingly different than the "unstyled" models they replaced. The most noticeable change was the addition of a radiator grille screen. The horizontally slatted screens contributed greatly to making the tractors look rugged, and they also helped prevent

buildup of foreign materials—such as straw, weeds, and dirt—around the steering pedestal and in front of the radiator.

The steering pedestal was also redesigned to complement the look of the grille screens. The nonconvex-pentagonal shape of the pedestal's front (which was all that one could see now with the grille screens present) gave the tractors a more determined look, if you will. The shape of the front of the pedestal graciously curved up over the top of the grille screens, over the steering gear, and ran all the way back over the length of the newly designed hood, corresponding beautifully with the new pedestal and grille.

The styled A also sported newly positioned stacks. Dreyfuss located both pipes in line with

Not only did Deere make the A more attractive at a distance by styling it, the company also made the tractors more operator-friendly. For instance, the gauges were located on a new dashboard behind the fuel tank, making them easier for the operator to read. Additionally, a gearshift quadrant was adopted, which made it easier for one to see what gear the tractor was in.

the center of the hood, with the exhaust pipe out front. Additionally, the air intake was made to resemble the shape of the exhaust, providing symmetry in their design. An operator would only have to look around one obstruction with this new centrally positioned arrangement. Some of the new A's other appearance improvements included the steering gear height being lowered 1 23/32 inches and reduced in size. Additionally, the height of the exhaust and air intake stacks was reduced by 4 inches, giving the tractor a more sleek, finished appearance.

Deere also added an instrument panel to the styled A. Located right behind the fuel tank and flowing out of the shape of the hood, the new instrument panel contained the water temperature gauge, oil temperature gauge, the three-way fuel valve control, and the shutter control. Dreyfuss had made sure that all of the controls on the stylized As were easy to reach and operate. Furthermore, the purpose of each control was made easier to understand by its shape, location, and, in some rare instances, labeling.

The 1939 Model As also introduced a newly designed front end and frame. According to Decision 7750, the front pedestal was 2 3/4 inches further forward, boosting the wheelbase of the tractor from 87 5/16 inches to 90 1/16 inches. Due to this lengthened front end, the strength of the side frame rails needed to be reinforced. Thus, the thickness of the frame rails increased from 1/2 to 5/8 inch, widening the front end by half an inch.

In relation to the unstyled models, the early styled Model As had hood decals in the same general location, but the letter style and size had been changed. Furthermore, the "General Purpose" lettering had been eliminated. And, in order to compensate for covering the radiator top tank by the grille screens, Deere placed a "medallion" transfer on the new nose cone of the more modern tractors. One thing that did stay the same from the latter unstyled tractors and the early styled tractors, though, was the use of the model designation stencil on the seat support channel. Just as on the unstyled models, this stencil was to be placed such that it was readable downhill from the clutch pulley side of the tractor.

By placing the exhaust and air intake stacks in line with one another, Deere improved the tractor operator's forward view. For a restoration to be accurate to the original design, both stacks need to be the same height.

Some decal sets for the styled As feature the "A-in-circle" decal. That decal, which was placed in the recessed area of the grille screen on the late-styled A row-crops, was never used on the early styled tractors are far as is known. Instead, those tractors featured the model designation stenciled on the seat support channel.

The front-end cross angle was increased from 5 to 6 inches in depth to improve the front end's strength. Furthermore, the new As featured a repositioned toolbox; it was now attached to the horizontal portion of the right-side frame rail.

Largely due to the presence of the new grille screens, Deere also increased the front-facing area of the radiator so that adequate cooling could be provided. The company chose to continue using the Modine Hy-Flow core, but the number of full-length tubes increased by 7, to 89. All in all, the front-facing dimensions of the radiator changed from 18 1/2x16 9/16 inches to 20x17 1/8 inches, increasing the total frontal area from almost 306.5 square inches to about 357.5 square inches. The

Seen here is the new high-backed seat, the round-spoke steering wheel, and the correct placement of the model designation on the seat support channel. That stencil was to be placed such that it was readable downhill from the clutch pulley side of the tractor.

44207-G

This factory photo of a long-hood A with starting and lighting equipment and pressed steel wheels gives us some ideas about a number of things. For one, the "JOHN DEERE" on the hood is clearly a decal. But this tractor is unusual in that it has an unidentifiable decal just in front of the battery cover hood extensions. Also note that this tractor does NOT have the "MODEL A" stencil running down the seat support channel as is the norm. Instead, it simply has an "A" decal in a SQUARE, not a circle-as used on the grilles of the late-styled tractors. Also note that the exhaust stack on this unit appears to be painted green. *John Deere Archives*

The "JOHN DEERE" lettering on the rear of the rear axle housings of these tractors was originally painted yellow, and the rear axle shafts were painted black as seen on this tractor.

This wartime tractor is late enough that it could be fitted with electric starter and lights, but it does not have those popular options. Interestingly, though, it does have the optional fenders, an extra feature that is desirable on any row-crop A tractor.

new radiator also used a screw-on cap instead of the old bar and clamp–style cap.

To further reduce costs, Deere also employed the new United air cleaner in place of the old Vortox air cleaner at this time.

Mid-1939 Production Changes

Seeing a need for even stronger front pedestals on the A, Deere & Company published Decision 8148 on New Year's Eve Day in 1938 to do just that. This document stated that the new pedestals were strengthened beginning with the serial numbers listed in Table 9.

Decision 8014 of October 28, 1938, ordered that the A2111 (A2111R) radiator grille screen

screening material be changed from wire mesh to perforated sheet steel. This went into effect on serial number A482365 on February 1, 1939.

At serial number 483326 on February 24, 1939, Deere began punching three 15/32-inch holes in each fan shaft support to provide a place to attach the generator bracket.

A Boost in Engine Size: The Changes Continue in 1940

Beginning with serial number 488000, the 1940 Model As also had their fair share of noteworthy changes. The most noticeable and important were those that Deere made to the engines. Most of the changes which occurred at this time

Rubber was used extensively by the United States in World War II, being used for making tires for aircraft and vehicles, among other things. Even though these are styled tractors, they are fitted with steel wheels likely as a result of wartime demand for rubber.

were the result of Deere's Decision 8550 dated September 5, 1939.

Engine

The new engines had an increased displacement of 321.2 cubic inches, caused by the 1/4-inch increase in stroke length. The new engine also had an improved head with a ramped design that increased the turbulence within the cylinders, which in turn helped the engines burn fuel more efficiently. The A's engine also featured a greater compression ratio, being raised from 3.9:1 to 4.45:1.

Not surprisingly, the bigger, better engines had more horsepower than their predecessors. Under rated load the new A produced 26.36 belt horsepower at the University of Nebraska, up from 23.63 rated load belt horsepower from the 1934 tests. To accommodate the increase in power, Deere fitted the A with different pistons, rings, and connecting rods.

The redesigned engine also had a number of far-reaching effects. The redesign caused changes

in the block, crankshaft, flywheel, manifold, manifold gaskets, head gaskets, valve guides, rocker arm cover, exhaust pipe, muffler, and even the bracket on the air cleaner. Indeed, just about the only things that weren't significantly influenced by the new engine were the petcocks, drain plug, fan support, spark plug wire shield, and a few other components. Even the spark plugs themselves were changed! Previously, Champion AC77L plugs, Edison Z88 hot plugs, or Auto-Lite TD-12 plugs had been used. The new plugs included Champion AC86 plugs and Autolite BD9 and BD12 plugs.

Magneto

Deere continued to use the Wico Type C magneto after A488000, but beginning with that tractor a different impulse drive angle was used, as were shorter lugs. To distinguish between the magnetos, Deere gave the new magneto a new part number: AH653R. The old magneto retained part number AB2875R.

Carburetor

The DLTX-18 carb was replaced by the DLTX-33 carburetor at this time.

Oil Filter and Pump

Deere also made a change to the oil filter element at serial number 488000. Replacing the original metal oil filter (AA357R) was a disposable paper filter element (AA3680R). This new element increased the time period between changes, improved efficiency, and reduced costs. The B2300R oil pump body also replaced the original B241R body, and included a new strainer screen.

The tail ends of 1943 and 1944 model tractors reveal several key details. The tractor on the left demonstrates the optional PTO, whereas the 1944 on the right is fitted with the optional Powr-Trol with PTO. The "Be Careful" decal on the tractor at left is likely close to the original location, though some tractors have that decal located a little higher. The "Powr-Trol" decal is in the correct, original location on the other tractor.

Fan

The new AA3659R fan took the place of the AA3673R fan.

Radiator and Shutters

To accommodate the increase in horsepower, an almost entirely new radiator assembly was introduced with A488000. This included the radiator core, sides, top and bottom tanks, fan shroud, and radiator shutter assembly.

Fuel Tank

Deere made a new fuel tank available for use on all-fuel powered tractors beginning with A488000. This new tank was accompanied by the small AA5554R gasoline-starting tank with fittings. Deere also employed new front and rear cushioned fuel tank supports for all fuel types at this time.

Final Drives and Rear Axles

The A3045R final drive gears took the place of the A3056R gears at this point, while new rear axles also came on the scene. The new rear axles necessitated the use of different hubs on wheels, though most wheels remained in service just using new hubs.

PTO

The PTO shaft also received a few changes at this time, as well. While its diameter increased from 1 1/8 inch to 1 3/8 inch, its operating speed slowed from 558 rpm to 546 rpm. Additionally, Deere discontinued the PTO shaft as standard equipment, making it available as special equipment.

Special Equipment: Tires

Other special equipment changes that Deere initiated on the A affected the tire sizes. The company dropped the 9.00x36-, 10.00x36-, and 11.25x36-inch special equipment rear tires in favor of the larger 9x38- and 10x38-inch low-pressure tires mounted on steel disc wheels. Additionally, Deere approved the use of the JD1242R heavy-duty-drive wheel for use on As, ANs, and AWs fitted with A2496R rear axles.

The rear axle shafts on this tractor are black, as they were on almost any styled A row-crop. Other parts that should be black are the tires, steering wheel grip, magneto cover, spark plug wires, and the exhaust stack. Also, the exhaust manifold was sometimes painted green, but the paint on that component typically burned away quickly due, thus many owners today opt to simply leave them untouched.

This factory photo of an early-styled A reveals a "SAFETY FIRST" transfer on the back of the seat, along with a transfer on the side of the Powr-Trol unit. Note also the black cased lights and the gauge rims which appear to be green in this photo. Also, this tractor has an unusual exhaust stack, but since this tractor has been in the field, some modifications may have been made to it. *John Deere Archives*

A very well-worn unit, this tractor is covered with decals. Below the part number on the lift unit is a transfer labeled "U.S.A. PAT." which then lists two patent numbers and then probably says "PAT'S P'ING." although that lettering is not totally legible. On the right-hand side of the unit is a similar transfer. Just above the part number on the lift unit is a barely visible "POWER LIFT" instructional transfer. Also just visible in this photo is the crankcase breather transfer. *John Deere Archives*

Overdrive

With Decision 9088, Deere approved the use of the AA2369R overdrive, which provided a 1:2.78 gear ratio in the row-crop Model As.

Mid-1940 Changes
Wheels

It is very unclear what happened to the wheels on the A at this point, as various sources conflict with one another. However, it does seem that some alterations were made in the available wheel equipment at some point during 1940 production. The affected wheels included the A1815R and A2366R cast disk wheels, as well as the B1545R and F337R wheels.

Steering Wheel

According to Decision 8935, the AA380R steering wheel had alterations made to its hub. Instead of the original cast hub with spokes riv-eted in, the hub was changed to plain round steel with spokes pressed in. This caused a change in the French & Hecht part number; the new number was #A-404-WG-508B, which replaced #A-337-WG-508B. This change occurred on A497407 in the summer of 1940, according to a Deere document.

Flywheel

Decision 8955 stated that the finger depressions in the A2237R flywheel would be removed, and the width of the flywheel rim would be increased from 1 to 1 1/8 inches. According to the Deere document, this change went into effect on A494416 in February 1940.

Oil Pump Stud

Deere shortened the oil pump stud from 10 1/4 inches to only 9 1/8 inches at A495960.

TABLE 10

Speeds of Row-Crop As with 6-Speed Transmissions
(in miles per hour as outlined in Decision 9420)

Models A, AN, and AW fitted with the following rear tire sizes:

Gear	9x38	10x38	11x38	12x38
First	2.36	2.47	2.55	2.61
Second	3.10	3.24	3.34	3.43
Third	4.04	4.22	4.36	4.47
Fourth	5.31	5.54	5.72	5.87
Fifth	7.09	7.40	7.64	7.84
Sixth	12.13	12.65	13.07	13.40
Reverse	3.75	3.92	4.05	4.15

Models ANH and AWH fitted with 9.00x40-inch rear tires:

First	2.61
Second	3.43
Third	4.47
Fourth	5.87
Fifth	7.84
Sixth	13.40
Reverse	4.15

Special Equipment: Tires

Deere's Decisions 9004 and 9186 approved two tire sizes as special equipment for the A, AN, and AW. The first decision allowed 10 x 36-inch six-ply rice-type tires and tubes to be used on tractors with the AA1002 demountable rim. The second decision gave approval for the use of 12 x 38-inch six-ply tires on 38x11-inch W-DW rims mounted on cast wheels. These decisions went into effect in January and April 1940, respectively.

1941 Brings More Changes

The most important changes that occurred at serial number 499000, at the beginning of 1941 Model A production, were to the transmission and related components.

Transmission

Deere eliminated the old four-speed transmission that the A had used since its introduction, supplanting it with a six-speed transmission that provided a greater range of speeds. In addition to requiring new slider gears and main case, there were a number of other internal and external changes which took place. The new six-speed transmission was to be only with rubber tires, as the increased speeds (as outlined in Deere's Decision 9420) were deemed too fast for steel wheels.

Gearshift

Deere accommodated an increase in the number of gears in the transmission by adding a gearshift quadrant and altering the gearshift lever. New shifter shafts and forks were also added.

Carburetor

After just one year of use, the DLTX-33 carburetor was supplanted by the DLTX-53 carburetor.

Standard Equipment: Rear Wheels

Decision 9403 of August 1, 1940, proclaimed that Models A, AN, and AW would thereafter be sold with pressed steel wheels as standard equipment. The standard rear tire for all three models was to be 9 x 38-inch four-plys. The A and AW would be fitted with 5.5 x 16-inch four-ply fronts standard; the AN would be fitted with 9 x 10-inch six-ply fronts standard. This decision, which went into effect on tractor A499000, was made because about 85 percent of all row-crop As sold since July 1939 had been fitted with full rubber tires.

Special Equipment: Rear Axles

The 96-inch-wide rear axles and special rear axle housings as used on the ANH tractors were made available as special equipment on the rest of the row-crop Model As by virtue of Decision 9742 of February 1941. That decision went into effect in February, even though it was a while after the A488000 changeover as shown in the parts books.

Mid-1941 Alterations
Lighting Equipment

Resulting from Deere's Decision 9330 of July 10, 1940, the last A to use 7-inch-diameter headlights was A500011; starting with A500012, Deere used 5-inch diameter headlights instead. Affected items included the black molding, lens and lens retaining spring, and bulb. At the same time the A2611R front-light mounting brackets replaced the D2914R brackets. Similarly, the rear-lamp mounting bracket changed from B1601R to A2612R. These changes also necessitated changes in the wiring harness.

Starter

The AA2004R/AA4929R Delco-Remy No. 000760 starter saw service on As up to serial number 502231, and were replaced by the AA3096R Delco-Remy No. 1108908 starter and the AA4930R Delco-Remy No. 1108914 starter at A502232. A Deere document accompanying Decision 9372 of July 9, 1940 (which announced this change), stated that the new AA3095R (possibly a typographical error actually meant to refer to number AA3096R) starters were also used on the Model As listed in Table 11. According to the parts books, Deere discontinued the use of the AA3096R starter at serial number 504141.

While it is often best to paint certain parts while they are off of the tractor, it is often necessary to "touch up" nuts and bolts, as the paint on those items often wears when they are being installed. It is important to remember that many of the components of the tractor were already assembled when it went into the company's paint booth.

Serial Number Plates

During World War II, the U.S. government restricted aluminum usage. Therefore, Deere published Decision 9861 on March 28, 1941, announcing that the next order of serial number plates was to be made with "strip steel with lead-tin alloy coating" made by a hot dip process. It is unclear when those new serial number plates first appeared on the A, however.

The War Years

Throughout the war years of 1941–1945, production of the Model A slowed and changes were few and far between.

1943: Fan Support

Following 250 scrapped serial number plates (which may have been scrapped in relation to Decision 9861, but the actual reason is unknown), A522600 was the first tractor to receive the A2830R fan support in place of the A844R support.

Table 11

Tractors Using the AA3095R Starter

500670	502186
500808	502188
501890	502189
501946	502190
501954	502193
501993	502194
501994	502195
501996	502196
502063	502208
502128	502210
502175	502212
502176	502217
502177	502228
502178	502229
502184	

1943: Power Shaft Related Components

At serial number 523600 a new PTO shaft was employed, making necessary the use of a new PTO housing seal. Deere also added a PTO flipper guard to the A at this time.

1943: Radiator Components and Heat Indicator

Beginning with serial number 523600, the A's radiator top tank switched from A2367R to A2906R, and the radiator bottom tank changed from A2368R to A2829R. At the same time, Deere also changed the flange filter, drain tube, and the radiator cap and its accompanying gasket to accommodate the new pressure cooling system. These changes required a new heat indicator.

1945: Radiator Components and Heat Indicator Changed Back

At the start of 1945 production, Deere switched back to using virtually all of the radiator components that had been replaced in 1943. Some additional small radiator parts were changed at this time as well.

1945: Fan Support Changed Back

After terminating its use in 1943, Deere went back to using the A844R fan support early in 1945 production at serial number 543000.

1945: PTO Shifter Lever

The PTO shifter lever on the row-crop As, beginning with serial number 545688, was part number A3057R, which took the place of the A2458R lever.

1945: Generator and Related Parts

At serial number 542718, Deere & Company dropped the Delco-Remy No. 1101356 and No. 1101385 generators, replacing them with Delco-Remy's No. 1101371 generator. This change sparked many others, as Deere altered the generator adjusting strap, belt, and generator-related washers and bolts at this time as well. Later generator-related changes in 1945 came with serial number 547261, when the B2124R generator drive pulley replaced the D2911R (AA1930R) pulley.

1945: Crankcase Breather

Other changes at A542718 occurred to the engine crankcase breather components, including both the breather body and stack.

1945: Fan and Fan Shaft

At serial number 547261, the A's fan assembly received extensive changes. The most important new parts were the A3663R shaft and the AA3717R fan.

1945: Brake Latch

A550066 was the first to use a new brake latch. Further examples of minor changes made during the war include the addition of a clip used on the wiring harness shield, a trash screen beneath the radiator, and a washer and nut on the light switch.

1946

Beginning with A561903, the A featured an improved drawbar assembly with a "bent" drawbar end.

Paint and Decals

There is no known evidence indicating that any of the row-crop Model As had a paint color combination other than the standard green bodies with yellow wheels. However, there were a number of changes in both the style and placement of decals and/or stencils on these tractors.

The original placement of decals on the styled As was determined by Decision 7750. Most of the information contained here was gleaned from that Deere document.

Fenders were an option on the row-crop As, and were painted John Deere green. The easiest way to properly paint these it to remove them from the tractor so that all places can be easily reached with paint.

Hood Decals

The B-1536 stencil was used on both sides of the A's hood and consisted of the words "JOHN DEERE" in 2 1/2-inch letters. These stencils were placed within the recess of the tractor's hood, with the lower edge of the letters 1/2 inch from the lower edge of the recess, with the front edge of the stencil located 11 inches behind the hood's leading edge.

Nose Cone "Medallion" Stencil

Deere's B-1537 stencil consisting of the words "JOHN DEERE" in 3/4-inch letters was placed 1 3/4 inches above the bottom edge of the nose cone (or "medallion") and 1 1/4 inches in from its side.

Model Designation Stencil

The A-1065 "Model A" stencil as used on the unstyled "A" continued in use on the early styled As and was placed in the same location on the seat support channel, readable downhill from the belt pulley side of the tractor.

"Leaping Deer" Stencil

On the early styled As, the 4 1/4-inch "Leaping Deer," stencil B-1538, appeared on the rear axle housing cover. Located in the center of that housing cover, the stencil's top was 6 inches from the top of the cover.

For tractors using the hydraulic power lifts, this stencil also appeared on the Power Lift valve housing. With its top spaced 3 inches from the top of that housing, the stencil was centered on that unit.

Since the rear of the fuel tank was no longer exposed as it was on the unstyled tractors, Deere dropped this stencil from use on the rear of the tank.

No "A-in-Circle" Used

Even though some people restore their early-styled As using decal sets that contain the "A" in the circle, that decal is not documented as ever having been used by the factory on these tractors.

It is always a good idea to either mask off the tires of a tractor before you paint its wheels or to paint the wheels before you put the tires on them. Doing so will help your tractor look as nice as this one.

Patent Transfers

Decision 9911 of May 9, 1941, stated that the borders on the A827R and A2252R transfers as used on the row-crop As would be changed from red to black. This was to go in effect on or before February 14, 1944.

Safety First Transfers

Decision 9078 outlined two "Safety First" transfers as to be used on the A series tractors. The first, A2568R, indicated that one of the transfers should be applied to the back of the seats on all tractors. This transfer, according to the decision, read "DRIVE TRACTOR AT SAFE SPEEDS. REDUCE SPEED WHEN TURNING OR APPLYING INDIVIDUAL BRAKES. DRIVE SLOWLY OVER ROUGH GROUND." The decision

does not indicate, however, if all of those letters were supposed to be capitalized or not.

The second transfer, which was to appear on the PTO shield "just ahead of the notch for attaching Implement Guard," was the A2569R transfer. It read "STOP POWER SHAFT BEFORE DISMOUNTING FROM TRACTOR." Again, though, all of those letters may not have been capitalized. Both of these decisions were put in effect on May 6, 1940.

Hood Transfer Changed

According to Deere documents, the hood stencil on the Model A was changed starting on September 5, 1940. The most notable difference was the addition of a black outline on the letters. Deere increased the height of the letters

The early styled As are very fine-looking tractors and are an important part of the model's history. These tractors also tend to be quite collectible since the bulk of their production years took place during World War II, a time when tractor production as a whole dwindled.

from 2 1/2 to 2 3/4 inches and increased the total length of this decalcomania transfer from about 23 5/8 to 25 1/2 inches, according to Deere documents. Decison 9406, which called for this branding change, also stated that this new A2645R brand was to be a decalcomania transfer, replacing the silk-screened B1536R.

"Medallion" Transfer Changed

The "medallion" decalcomania transfer located on the nose cone of the tractors was altered sometime in the spring of 1941. The transfer was shortened from about 7 11/32 inches to 6 3/8 inches, according to Deere documents, though the letter height and size remained unchanged. Additionally, the letters received black outlines, whereas before they were simply all yellow. This was the result of Decision 9590 of October 26, 1940.

Safety First Transfer Changed

Resulting from Decision 11317 of July 18, 1945, the A2658R Safety First transfer received a few changes. Instead of "Safety First," the new stencil read "Be Careful" and it no longer used the white cross on green background. Instead of white letters on the black background, the "Be Careful" A2568R stencil featured black letters on a white background. Another change included the replacement of the narrow gold border with a wider black-and-white border. The new "Be Careful" stencil also sported different dimensions, measuring 3 1/8 x 2 3/8 inches as opposed to 4 1/2 x 2 inches. This change was reportedly made to make the A2568R stencil the same size as the A2569R stencil. This decision was to go into effect with the next order, which was estimated to take place around mid-December 1945.

Chapter 4

The Late-Styled Model A Row-Crops

Decision 7750 had been a big one for the Model A as were the years 1940 and 1941. The stalwart Model A had undergone many changes indeed. Nevertheless, Decision 12000 would change the face of the A forever. One hundred sixteen pages long, the decision initiated most of its sweeping alterations to the model partway through the 1947 model year, beginning at serial number 584000.

AN and AW Changed:
ANH and AWH Eliminated

Deere & Company discontinued the ANH and AWH designations at this time, but the advantages of those models were not sacrificed. Instead, Deere updated the AN and AW to have the same features and advantages that made the ANH and AWH what they were. These new ANs and AWs sported revised ANH- and AWH-style rear axle housings as well as new cast disk drive wheels with offset centers. With that combination, both the AN and AW had rear tread adjustable from 56 to 104 inches.

In order to make the AN and AW more like the previous ANH and AWH, Deere made 42-inch rear tires standard on those models. These

The last major changes to the A occurred at serial number 584000, in the middle of the 1947 model year. By that time, the A looked vastly different from the original 1934 models which had started it all. And, indeed, it was very different.

tires provided a total clearance of 27 inches under the rear axle, but 38-inch rear tires were also available. This smaller tire provided only 25.3 inches of clearance. When fitted with the smaller tires, the AW had shorter front spindles while the AN was fitted with the old 9 x 10-inch front wheel instead of the now standard 7.5 x 16-inch front six-ply tire. Deere chose to discontinue the steel front wheel as optional equipment for the AN. This meant that both the AN and AW were available only on all-rubber tires.

Models AN and AW also introduced interchangeable front ends, made possible by a new two-piece front pedestal. Previous front pedestals had been of one-piece construction, with the entire pedestal extending from the steering gear all the way down to the front wheels. Those older pedestals connected to the tractor in numerous locations; thus if the farmer wished to change front ends on his or her A, it would be a major undertaking. But the new pedestal was a two-piece design—the top part of the pedestal, largely made up of casting A3277R, ran from the steering gear down to the bottom of the frame, while the lower part could be fitted with either the yoke for the AN's single front wheel, or the AW's wide adjustable front axle assembly. Thus, farmers could buy a Model AN and a separate wide front-end assembly for their tractor and could change the front end with little difficulty. In literature dating as early as October 1946, Deere advertised that one could change the front-end assemblies on this new front pedestal "in just a few minutes'

While it is very easy to tell and unstyled tractor from a styled one, it is a little more difficult to distinguish early-styled tractors from late-styled units. Perhaps the quickest way to do that is to look at the frame. With the drastic change in the design of the frame, from the early-styled's channel frame to late-styled's pressed steel frame, also came changes in decals and their placement. Note, however, that the tractor shown at the right is a later version of the late-styled A. Those tractors sported the "JOHN DEERE" hood decals further forward as seen here, while on the earlier late-styled tractors that decal was located in basically the same spot as it was on the early-styled As.

time." Because of the new front pedestal, however, one now shouldn't automatically assume that a 1947 and later A that looks like either an AN or an AW really is what it appears to be on the surface!

The A Undergoes a Major Facelift

Most of the changes that occurred to the Model A in 1947 were the result of Decision 12000. Unless otherwise noted, the changes listed here occurred at serial number 584000 during the 1947 production year.

Frame

One of the most noticeable changes to the A

at this time was the elimination of the cast steel frame. The new pressed steel frame was used to both improve the tractor's appearance and reduce cost. This change affected a number of other components, which are explained later.

Flywheel Cover, Flywheel, and Related Parts

Since the electric starting motor was standard equipment on these tractors, Deere gave the new As a totally enclosed flywheel. The new flywheel cover was great from the safety perspective, as there was no exposed portion of the flywheel. Deere's foresight in designing the new flywheel cover permitted an operator to start the tractor even if the electric starter failed. Deere provided a round cover, located at the center of the main fly-wheel cover, that could be moved out of the way if necessary, giving access to a place where a special manual cranking tool could be inserted. The operator simply inserted the tool, attached a steering wheel to it, gave the wheel a turn (just like he or she would have done to the old exposed flywheels), and got back to work. The cover between the flywheel and the main case was also new to A584000.

Seat: From Steel to Cushions

Perhaps the best change from the operator's perspective, the A's steel pan seat was replaced by a cushioned "battery box" seat with a padded backrest. The seat—which was adjustable both forward and backward over a 5-inch range—was mounted in a steel frame that sat upon a steel open-topped box containing the battery. The new battery box featured a slight indenture in the rear that was used for mounting the rearward-facing light. Mounted atop the Powr-Trol unit, the battery box did not take up any space on the platform like the previous seat support body did, so the operator enjoyed more legroom.

Gearshift Quadrant and Transmission Cover

While the quadrant itself was not changed, it was rotated forward to provide additional legroom and clearance for the new overdrive shifter handle. This rotation required a change in the transmission top cover and also in the related gaskets.

It is interesting to note that the majority of the changes that took place on the A at this time simultaneously occurred on the Model B, and vice versa. The B, however, received an entirely new gearshift quadrant, which provided locations for all six forward gears, thus eliminating the need for the overdrive lever. It was some time,

The late-styled As were the first to use the "A-in-circle" decal. The "A" was yellow on a black background, and the decal was placed in the recessed area of the grille screens on both sides of the tractor, just as on this tractor.

Model ANs and AWs that feature the pressed steel frame came standard with rather tall 42-inch rear wheels, a feature that makes these tractors' stature look almost identical to that of the previous Models ANH and AWH, respectively.

however, before this change took place on the A.

Steering Shaft Support

While the previous support had been a simple tube, the new A3350R steering shaft support looked more stylish and fit in better with the appearance of the pressed steel frame and

Deere maintained the 38-inch rear rubber as an option for the Models AN and AW, and it appears that the AW (above) took advantage of that option. The AN (below), however, is using the 42-inch standard tires, though (since these tires are so hard to find) they are not of the correct 45-degree lug type.

Much like on the unstyled AWs, the styled AWs had the front axle sticking out in front of the tractor. This caused the front wheels to be further forward on this model than they were on the basic A.

By giving the AN and AW the features of the ANH and AWH as standard equipment, that allowed Deere to eliminate the ANH and AWH from their line.

This AN has the "A-in-circle" decal in the correct place, and the air intake and exhaust stacks are painted as the originals were. Also, the wheel hubs on this tractor are entirely yellow while the axle shafts are black-an original and correct combination.

When viewing an A from the rear, the quickest ways to tell a late-styled A from an early-styled model is to look for the battery box seat and the absence of the words "JOHN" and "DEERE" cast into the rear axle housings.

totally enclosed flywheel.

Front Pedestal

The new As also sported a new front pedestal. According to Deere's Decision 12000, this pedestal boosted the vertical clearance above the front tires from 15/16 inch to 2 1/16 inches. This change gave the Model A a more "nose-up" appearance and improved crop clearance. Note the changes to Models AN's and AW's front pedestals as discussed earlier.

Roll-O-Matic Front End (Optional)

For the conventional As with dual, narrow-set front wheels in the tricycle configuration, Deere offered a new, impressive option in 1947: the revolutionary Roll-O-Matic front-end assembly. This system was unique to John Deere tractors, and it made operation smoother in all conditions. When any one of the tractor's front wheels encountered an obstruction or change in land contour that was less than or equal to 5 inches in height, the wheel raised up in relation to the front pedestal assembly while the other

front wheel lowered the exact same distance. This operation was made possible by the Roll-O-Matic's internal gears and knuckles. One of the main benefits of the Roll-O-Matic was that it caused the tractor's front end to raise *half* the distance it would have had it been equipped with the conventional, rigid front-end assembly.

The Roll-O-Matic could be fitted to tractors as early as 1939 models, thus it appears in the parts books on tractors back to A477000. However, this was not an original option on the early-styled As, so probably none of those tractors left the factory with the Roll-O-Matic. It is likely, though, that some of those earlier tractors sport this feature because of later add-ons.

Main Case

A584000 also debuted a drastically redesigned main transmission case. The new case, A3290R, was designed such that only a portion of the front of the case was machined flat. Additionally, the starter hole was relocated to beneath where the flywheel attached, thus requiring a new plate to be mounted on the bottom of the case for access to the starter. The area in which the starter mounted was enclosed from above and the sides such that no engine crankcase oil would interfere with its operation. The numerous other differences between this case and the preceding A2644R case also largely related directly to the differences in the attached parts.

First Reduction Gear Cover

As a result of changes in the main case, Deere designed a new first reduction gear cover (A3263R), which began use at A584000 in the 1947 model year. Accompanying the new cover was a new pulley shield.

Rear Axle Housings

While there had been a few changes to the rear axle housings over the years, the one that was most noticeable—at least from a distance— occurred with A584000: the words "JOHN" and "DEERE" were no longer cast into the left and right rear axle housings, respectively. The new A3270R housing replaced the original A1866R

housing, which had been in use since the beginning of A production (even though a few changes had been made to it in that time).

Engine: The New Cyclone

The new Cyclone engine was available in two different, specially designed types. One was the time-tested all-fuel design, while the other was for gasoline only. Both types had their own pistons, the all-fuel version using the A3281R pistons and the gasoline version using the A3282R pistons. The gasoline version could even be fitted with special high-altitude A4786R pistons. While the Model A's engine retained the 5 1/2 x 6 3/4-inch bore and stroke, the new pistons were longer and thus increased the compression ratio and, as a result, power.

The Cyclone engines featured refined combustion chambers that better controlled turbulence of the air-fuel mixture. The better consistency of that mixture allowed for better combustion, creating more efficient engines.

The engine changes were extensive. The new A3462R cylinder block featured a new pet-

It doesn't matter whether your late-styled A is the basic A, an AN, or an AW, it should have the nose cone medallion transfer on it. The grille screens were originally painted green, including the screened portion, and the exhaust stacks were finished in black, as well.

The most popular front tire style used on the A was the tri-rib type. Other styles were used as well, though.

cock location on the bottom. This was a result of the new pressed steel frame, an item that basically covered the entire side of the engine and thus made servicing more difficult. Other new parts included the different manifolds for the different engine types (including a cold manifold), the A3367R and A4226R cylinder heads, and the valve cover. Also new were the A3322R crankshaft, the roll pin, the A3265R left-hand main bearing housing, and the related engine gaskets.

Carburetor

Deere & Company used two new carburetors with improved calibration for these engines. The gasoline versions used the DLTX-71 carburetor, while the all-fuel As used the DLTX-72.

These new carburetors featured new choke levers and related components,   as well.

Air Cleaner

A new air cleaner assembly adorned the A at this point, with new components including the air stack, air cleaner bracket, the air cleaner itself, and the oil cup.

Starter

The starter became standard equipment on the Model A at this point. Replacing the optional Delco-Remy No. 1108914 starting motor at this time was the Delco-Remy No. 1108950 12-volt starter. Also new to this starter was the operating rod and pedal. The starter was relocated to beneath the flywheel of the tractor and enclosed in a separate compartment in the bottom of the main case.

Generator

Appearing at serial number 584000, the Delco-Remy No. 1101777 and 1100955 generators bearing Deere part number AA4921R accommodated the A's 12-volt system. These generators would remain all but unchanged until the end of A production, with only two changes occurring to them later.

To correctly restore a 1947 or later Model AN to the original configuration, one must make sure that the wheel combinations are correct. If your tractor sports the standard 42-inch rear tires, it should have the 7.50x16 front wheel with tire as shown here. However, if your tractor has the optional 38-inch rear tires, it should have the 9.00x10 front wheel and tire like that that came standard on the pre-1947 ANs.

Voltage Regulator

To control generator output, Deere employed the 1118792, 1118266, or 1118306 voltage regulators on the 12-volt Model A.

Radiator and Radiator Shutter Controls

The radiator bottom tank was redesigned to accommodate changes to the frame. Extensive changes took place to the radiator shutter controls at this time, as well, with alterations occurring to the control rod, handle control, and related components.

Toolbox

Also affected by the frame change was the toolbox. The new AA4760R toolbox remained in use until serial number 655194 in the 1950 model year.

Drawbar Assembly

Because of its welded, one-piece design, the A's new drawbar support was quite a bit stronger than the previous bolted-together assembly had been. The drawbar itself featured a vertical bend that allowed two different operating heights by simply pulling the pin, sliding the drawbar out of the frame, flipping it over, sliding it back in, and replacing the pin. That same pin was all that had to be removed in order to alter how far the drawbar stuck out, as there were a few adjustment holes located along its length. Like its predecessor, this drawbar was of the swinging type.

Hydraulics: The New Powr-Trol

Replacing the conventional Power Lift-type system that had been used on the Model A for over a decade, the new Powr-Trol was a much more effective, efficient system. The most important new aspect of the Powr-Trol was that it could regulate the depth of both mounted and drawn equipment, whereas the previous Power Lift simply raised or lowered the implement all the way up or down. As a result there was no provision for intermediate depths with the old system.

The new abilities of the lift system changed

Above and below: From 1947 until sometime in the 1950 model year, these tractors had their "JOHN DEERE" hood decals located in the center of the hood sides; later tractors had that decal positioned further forward, probably in an attempt to improve the appearance of the tractor.

the way in which it was operated. To raise or lower implements with the Power Lift, the operator simply kicked a pedal; one kick lowered the implement all the way, while the next kick raised it all the way. With the Powr-Trol, which needed a provision for specific depth control, Deere located a handle on the operator's left side to control the

When painting this tractor, the owner probably had the headlight lenses masked off. Also, the location of the John Deere emblem on the front center of this tractor's battery box is correct to original configuration.

Black headlight bodies, black steering wheel grip, and black gauge rings with the faces not painted-this tractor has been restored very well in respect to original appearance.

Powr-Trol. Simple forward and backward motions of the handle raised and lowered implements, with the central position of the lever's range of motion being neutral.

Deere's Powr-Trol was immensely successful and immediately popular, so much so that Deere apparently experienced problems producing enough of them to meet demand. It is obvious that the company must have anticipated this shortcoming; as early as October 1946, Deere advertising literature stated, "Insofar as production facilities will permit, the new Models 'A' and 'B' will be equipped with the Powr-Trol. Where Powr-Trol cannot be supplied, the regular hydraulic power lift will be furnished, and conversion assemblies will be made available at a later date if desired." Thus, it is likely that some 1947 model tractors left the factory with the old

power lift system instead of the Powr-Trol.

Other Changes to the Late-Styled As
1949: Deere made changes to the fan shaft and fan keeper with A632780.
1949: A635656 was the first to use only two of the 1/2-inch 12H13R lock washers on the upper water pipe, whereas previous tractors had used four. Those two washers were used only on the rear cap screw, while two new A3105R washers were used on the front cap screw.
1950: Farmers liked the single gear shift lever with quadrant that provided shifting into all six gears, which had been used on the Model Bs since the 1947 model year. Deere incorporated this feature on the Model A partway through 1950 model year production, at serial number 648000. This added feature caused drastic changes in the transmission compo-

Steering wheels on these tractors often have cracked rubber or the rubber has become "dead," often resulting in black hands after one has touched the steering wheel. Some places re-cover these steering wheels, but you need to make sure that they cover the wheels correctly, as other tractor manufacturers used different style steering wheels.

The telescoping front axle on the AW can sometimes fall victim to wear of paint if the owner has changed the front wheel spacing of the tractor since it has been painted. Such minor use-related wear should not be too harshly criticized.

While sometimes overlooked, there should be a "JOHN DEERE" decal on the back of the backrest on the late-styled As. Also, the rear lamp should have a black body with the lens masked off when being painted.

nents, both internal and external, as well as the transmission case top cover. Further changes also occurred to the differential "bull" gear, bevel pinion, and thrust washers.

1950: The power take-off and power lift were also the object of changes made in 1950.

1950: Deere extended the advantages of the interchangeable front ends of Models AN and AW to the basic Model A at this time. With this change, *any* row-crop A could be fitted with the dual wheel tricycle front end, the single wheel front end, or the adjustable wide front end. Furthermore, earlier tractors that were originally ANs or AWs could be fitted with the new A4041R housing for the dual-wheeled tricycle front end. Thus, that front end appears in the parts books as being available back to A584000 in 1947.

1950: A new toolbox appeared at A655194.

1950: Serial number 655572 marked the beginning of the use of the A3295R instrument panel on the gasoline-powered Model A.

1951: Replacing the old B2124R generator drive pulley at A674342 was the new

B2874R pulley.

1952: Deere and Company placed a new crankcase ventilator pump cover on the A at serial number 692121, as well as a new ventilator rote, roller, and gasket. Also changed at this point was the fan shaft rear bearing housing.

1952: The Model A underwent a few more changes quite late in 1952 production at serial number 700200, fewer than 3,200 tractors before the termination of A row-crop production. These changes included a new radiator tank bottom, water pipe, and accompanying radiator hose, along with the radiator hose clamps. At this same time, a water pump became standard equipment on the Model A, thus requiring a change in the A's frame.

Paint and Decals
"A-in-Circle" Begins Usage,
Stencil A-1065 Dropped

With the addition of the battery box seat and the elimination of the seat support channel, the

The late-styled As marked the end of an era for John Deere, but the A's influence on the company would last for many more years. The A's replacement was the Model 60, and the basic design of the A would remain in use through the Model 630.

original A-1065 model designation stencil was dropped. To fulfill the purpose of that stencil, however, Deere started placing the popular A-in-circle stencil, A3395R, on both grille screens of the tractor, centrally located in the recess in the side of each.

Battery Box Transfer

The JD122 transfer was to be moved from the rear axle housing cover to the front side of the battery box, where it was to be centrally located.

Seat Back Support Transfer

The JD113 stencil consisting of the words "JOHN DEERE" appeared on the new seat back support facing the rear.

Safety First Transfer

Due also to the elimination of the pan seat setup, the previous A2568R Safety First/Be Careful transfer, which had appeared on the back of that seat, was no longer placed there. Instead, Deere positioned it on the back side of the new steering shaft support. The bottom edge of this transfer was to be located 1/2 inch from the bottom of that support.

Powr-Trol Transfer

With Decision 12492, dated November 7, 1946, Deere indicated that the changes to the surface of the Power-Trol unit would be made in order to allow a decalcomania transfer to be added. The Power-Trol decal was to be attached to the tractor's "Power Control Valve Housing after tractor is painted." This went into effect on February 3, 1947.

Special Paint Instructions

To prevent rusting of certain parts, Deere published a decision on March 11, 1947, instructing that all parts surfaces that the flywheel cover covered (except the moving parts of the starter and the flywheel teeth) were to be painted. This decision, apparently retroactive, went into effect on Valentine's Day 1947, according to Deere documents.

Hood Decals

The hood decals on the Model A were moved forward during the 1950 model year.

Chapter 5

The Model AH (A Hi-Crop)

For the 1950 model year, John Deere introduced an upstanding—or, more accurately, a "tall standing"—version of the A: the Model AH Hi-Crop. The AH was designed for use in tall or high-bedded crops such as cane fields. Deere documents dated July 14, 1950, state that this tractor was "designed primarily for use in the territories of [Deere's] Atlanta, St. Louis, and San Francisco branches." While this model was very similar to the basic row-crop Model A, the AH did have a few distinguishing features. Not surprisingly, the majority of those related to the high-clearance aspect of the unit.

The A Hi-Crop gave 32 inches of clearance beneath the center of its rear axle, making this model quite adaptable for use in both tall crop and cane fields. Using the same engine as the basic A, the AH was also available with either gasoline or all-fuel engines and had similar horsepower performance relative to the basic A. AHs came standard with distributor ignition, but a high-tension magneto ignition was optional.

Deere advertised this model as both the "Model 'AH' Hi-Crop Tractor" and "The Famous Model 'A' On Stilts," beginning in 1950.

Standard Features

The AH had most of the same mechanical features of the basic A, so primarily the differences between those models are outlined here.

Rear Axles and Tread

Providing the increased clearance under the rear end were the new rear axle housings. These housings were fitted with new drop-box-style axle housings, which contained final drives. Two

This tractor shows just how tall the Model AH was. One must be careful when getting onto, off of, or simply operating this tractor, as a fall from that height would be quite dangerous.

While the Models ANH and AWH had been high-clearance tractors, the Model AH was a true hi-crop tractor. It provided an astounding 32 inches of clearance and is one of the most striking derivatives of the A series.

TABLE 12
The AH at a Glance

Width: 83 to 102 3/8 inches
Length: 152 1/2 inches
Height (overall): 97 inches
Height (to radiator cap): 78 inches
Height (of PTO): 36 3/8 inches
Weight: 6,400 pounds (approx.)

roller chains and sprockets transmitted the power from the differential to the driveshafts. Deere spaced the drop housings apart such that there was 48 inches of crop clearance between them. According to a Deere publication, the company deemed that spacing suitable for all possible applications of the AH through a series of testing and development.

Various set spacings of the rear wheels were possible with this setup. Set 6 inches apart, the available spacings were 60, 66, 72, 78, 84, and 90 inches. Operators could change those spacings, not by moving the wheel on the axle as on most Deeres of that era, but by changing the rear wheels' and hubs' positions. This arrangement

One striking feature of the AH is its different rear wheel type. With these wheels, rear wheel spacings in 6-inch increments were available from 60 to 90 inches.

All AHs were produced late enough that they should have most of the same features as the late-styled Model A row-crops.

eliminated the need for long rear axle shafts protruding from the wheels, thus helping reduce the chance of damage to crops.

Front Axles and Tread

The AH's adjustable-width front axle used longer knees, affording 33 1/4 total inches of clearance under it. Like the rear axles, the front axle had available spacings in 6-inch increments. On the front axle, however, those spacings ranged from only 60 to 84 inches; the 90-inch spacing was not available.

Deere designed the front axle to oscillate quite a bit for use over rough terrain. With the axle at its narrowest setting, either front

The standard front tire size for the AH was 7.5 x 20-inch four-ply tires. Deere did not use a larger front tire size because it did not want them to appear "out of proportion."

Deere's AH came with two headlights and one rear lamp, all of which originally had black bodies and lenses, which were masked off.

As for rear tires, the standard size was 11x38-inch six-plys, but 12x38-inch tires were optional, as were 12x38-inch rice-and-cane rears.

wheel could raise 20 1/2 inches; with the axle in the wide setting, that distance increased to 28 1/2 inches.

Adjustable-Height Drawbar

The AH's "Easy-On, Easy-Off" drawbar was adjustable, with three set heights available. The lowest setting—14 inches—provided a straight

The location of the "Be Careful" decal on this tractor is accurate, as that decal appears in that location on almost all factory photos and advertising literature for this model.

Just as on the row-crop models, the Model AH should have the "JOHN DEERE" nose cone medallion decal in the location illustrated here.

Seen here are the correctly unpainted spark plugs and the clear sediment bowl. Also, note that the exhaust manifold on this tractor was once painted, but the paint has started to burn off.

All AHs were produced late enough that they should probably have the "JOHN DEERE" hood decal placed farther forward, just as on the row-crop models of this era. However, there are almost always exceptions to the rule.

line of draft for plowing and was recommended for use when pulling heavy loads. The middle setting—25 inches—was to be used for lighter loads. And, finally, the highest setting—32 inches—was supplied for use with sprayers and other such machines, which had high hitches.

But the specialization of the AH's drawbar didn't end there. A special narrow setting of the drawbar could be used in extreme conditions where there was a threat of mud or trash buildup between the drawbar and rear axle drop boxes. This setting, however, required the use of the high vertical setting. Additionally, one could remove the drawbar of the A Hi-Crop rather quickly, which might need to be done to obtain maximum clearance under the tractor.

Tires

Deere offered three options for the AH's rear tires: the first two options were regular-type tires, 11x38 inches and 12x38 inches, and the third option was rice and cane–type tires, 12x38 inches; all were rated six-ply. These rear tires, coupled with the A's six-speed transmission, gave the AH a range of speeds from about 1 1/2 to 12 miles per hour. Front tires were 7.50x20-inch standard four-ply.

Special Equipment

A hi-crop tractor required specialized implements as well. John Deere & Company wasted no time in marketing special hi-crop imple-

Yet another factory photo of the same preproduction AH, this photo clearly shows the forward location of the "JOHN DEERE" decals, as was normal for all A row-crops at this time. Strangely, though, the "A-in-circle" decal is not in the normal location; instead, it is toward the center of the nonrecessed area of the grille screen sides. Other notable items on this tractor are the exhaust stack, which appears to be green instead of black, and the outward-facing decal on the air cleaner. *John Deere Archives*

This rear-quartering view of the AH is dated March 1950, so this is a preproduction tractor. Nonetheless, much can be learned from this tractor. Note the placement of the seat backrest decal and the two "BE CAREFUL" decals as located on the back of the battery box and on the top of the PTO shield. Also, notice that the gauge outer rings are painted green, not black, and that the exhaust manifold is also painted green. Also notable is the absence of the "Powr-Trol" decal. *John Deere Archives*

ments. In addition to other special equipment, a few of the implements available for the Model AH included the following:

The Model HC-42 Tool Bar

Available in widths of 48, 78, and 120 inches, the HG-42 tool bars were the foundation for many implements used on the AH. Items that could be mounted on it included chisel cultivators, sweeps, and coil-spring cultivators.

The Model AG250 High-Clearance Cultivator

This unit could serve as either a one- or two-row cultivator. As a one-row, it could cultivate 60- to 84-inch rows; as a two-row, it could cultivate 30- to 42-inch rows.

Paint and Decals

The paint and decal schemes used on the AH were basically the same as those used on the row-crop As of the same era. Please see chapter 4 for further information on those changes.

The Model AH is by far the tallest of the A series tractors, standing 97 inches at its highest point, according to Deere literature.

Chapter 6

The Unstyled Models AR and AO

Not long after introducing the Model A as a row-crop tractor, Deere saw a need for a standard-tread tractor that was smaller than the company's Model D. Thus, experimentation on a standard-tread version of the A began. According to Deere & Company's Decision 5100 of January 3, 1935, that tractor would be the "Model As Standard Tread Tractor." The decision stated that this tractor was being designed in order to replace both the GP and GP Orchard with a single tractor design.

The new tractor, which would eventually be designated Model AR, had many advantages over its predecessors. For one, it had both a low manufacturing cost for Deere and a low operating cost for farmers. Weighing in at around 3,800 pounds dry weight, this model featured a lightweight design, low center of gravity, and proper weight distribution, all of which helped improve performance.

This standard-tread A was vastly different from its row-crop counterpart. It had shorter rear axle housings, a revised transmission case, and a shorter fan shaft. The controls were also altered in order to best work with the standard-tread design, including lengthening and strengthening the clutch rod and a change in the gearshift quadrant and its location. These tractors also featured shorter fuel tanks, made possible by the elimination of the taper on the sides, with an increased capacity of 17 gallons.

Above: The AR's front tread was set at 48 inches, while its rear tread was 51 inches. It had a wheelbase of 76 inches and an overall length of 124 inches. This slow-turning tractor, with a 13-foot turning radius, weighed in around 2 tons.

Left: The most popular standard-tread version of the Model A was known as the Model AR. Deere produced the AR, a tractor that competed with Deere's D in the wheatland-type tractor market, in this unstyled form from 1935 to 1949.

Standard Features

Standard equipment on the AR also helped make this model ideal for use in wheatland and orchard conditions. Much of this information comes from Deere's Decision 5100.

Engine

The AR used the same 309-cubic-inch engine utilized in the row-crop A tractors.

Four Forward Speeds

According to Decision 5100, this tractor's four-speed transmission would provide speeds of 1.97, 3.08, 4.05, and 6.35 miles per hour with the standard-equipment 1:2.05 overdrive transmission; the standard reverse speed would be 3.12 miles per hour.

Wheels and Tread

The rear wheels at introduction were 42 3/4x10-inch steel wheels standard. With those wheels mounted in the standard position, the AR

The rear wheels on the unstyled AR could be fitted with a variety of lug types. Perhaps the most popular were the "A"-shaped lugs shown here. Other optional lugs included spade lugs, button lugs, cast cone lugs, and very unusual-looking "road lugs" and "sand lugs."

On the early ARs, steel wheels came as standard equipment. Special steel wheel equipment for the rear wheels included extension rims, grousers, road bands, and rear wheel scrapers. For the front wheels, both guide bands and extension rims were available.

had a 50 5/8-inch rear tread width. However, reversing the wheels gave a wider tread width of 54 1/8 inches. The standard front wheels were 28x6-inch steel wheels, which provided a front tread of about 48 inches; the front wheels sported dust-proof bearings, as well.

Belt Pulley

The AR's belt pulley had a large belt pulley with a 12 13/16-inch diameter and 7 3/8-inch face according to advertising literature A-199-35-1. Since the AR's belt pulley was located on the end of the crankshaft, the pulley operated at 975 rpm; with its size, it provided a belt speed of 3,270 feet per minute. Deere advertised the AR as suitable for operation of a 24-inch John Deere thresher or 22-inch threshers produced by Deere's competitors.

Power Take-Off

Established as standard equipment on this model by Decision 5100, the AR's 1 1/8-inch splined power take-off shaft ran at 544 rpm.

The Model AO Introduced

Decision 5530 of May 28, 1935, announced that a new version of the standard-tread Model AR would be produced. Deere stated that the new version would use the Model AO designation in order "to provide for a single specification" for that version of the model. In actuality, the AO was almost identical to the Model AR, differing primarily by having steering brakes and a low air stack with a side outlet muffler. This model went into production less than a hundred tractors after production of the AR had started, and both models utilized the same serial number run.

The Standards (and Options) Are Changed
Rear Tires (Optional Equipment)

Starting June 1, 1935, 12.75x24-inch rear tires became optional for the AR.

Air Cleaner

The Vortox air cleaner on these tractors received a new body and cup starting with number 251378.

Major Changes at Serial Number 251486

The standard-tread versions of the Model A underwent extensive changes at this time midway through the 1936 model year.

Main Case, Main Bearing Housing, Oil Pump, Countershaft, and Brakes

While Deere revised the transmission main case on the row-crop As at the beginning of 1936, the main case on standard treads was not changed until this time, along with the left-hand main bearing housing. Just as on the row crops, changes to the oil pump affected the standards at this time. Additionally, the countershaft and related components were changed, as were the rear brake housings and brake shaft.

Fan Shaft

The length of the fan shaft was increased from 37 9/16 inches to 38 1/2 inches.

Magneto and Spark Plug Conduit

While Deere changed the magneto on the AR from the Fairbanks-Morse Type RV2A to the Type RV2B at this time, it also added a spark plug cable conduit to those tractors. New left-hand-side spark plugs, which had been increased in length from 25 1/2 inches to 27 1/2 inches as a result of Decision 5785, were also used.

The unstyled AO was very well suited for orchard work, with its intake and exhaust stacks eliminated. This particular example is a 1944 model.

Governor and Control Rods

Deere installed an almost entirely newly designed governor on the AR and AO tractors. Changes were also made to the speed control rods and the throttle rod at the same time.

Radiator Top Tank

The front edge of the radiator top tank was lowered by 1/8 inch as the result of Decision 5777. This decision was intended to improve the steering worm gear housing clearance on the row-crop tractors, but these re-designed radiator top tanks were also used on the standard-tread tractors as well, first appearing at serial number 251539.

Heat Indicator

Deere added a Stewart-Warner heat indicator to Models AR and AO at serial number 251668 as the result of Decision 5878, which also affected the row-crop As.

Rear Wheel Placement/Tread

Originally, the AR's standard-equipment rear wheels were supposed to be mounted on the tractor in the "regular" position, which provided a rear tread width of 50 5/8 inches. However, with that placement, there was little clearance between the rear wheels and the belt pulley. So, Deere announced on December 17, 1935, that the rear wheels should, as standard practice, be placed in the original "reverse" position to provide a standard rear tread of about 54 inches and more space between the rear wheels and the belt pulley. This went into effect on tractor 251794.

Oil Filter

Further changes were made to the oil filter head, head cover, and oil pressure valve spring with tractor 251821.

Rear Wheels (Optional Equipment)

Originally, Deere had used the A1106R rear drive wheels with cast rims, but changing the tires on those rims proved to be too difficult. Thus, Deere issued Decision 5947 in December 1935 to announce the discontinuation of that wheel as optional equipment. Replacing it was the A1272R wheel with demountable rim, and this went into effect on tractor 251858 in January 1936.

Hood Shields for Model AO

Decision 5898 of November 8, 1935, announced the adoption of new hood shields to cover the fuel and gas tank caps, as well as a new AA887 air stack assembly and AA888 exhaust opening cover. These changes went into effect on tractor 251972.

Front Axle

In Decision 5979, Deere announced alterations in the design of the front axle of both the AR and AO in order to improve its strength. The new front axle first appeared on tractor 251974.

Mud Scrapers

Deere authorized use of mud/wheel scrapers for both regular drive wheels and extension rims with Decision 5909 in November 1935, a change that first affected tractor 252199. The following earlier tractors also benefited from this decision.

Mud Guards

Decision 5924 of December 3, 1935, which went into effect on January 10, 1936, approved the use of mud guards on the rear axle outer bearings of these tractors.

Seat

Clearly showing John Deere's concern for its customers' well-being, the company published Decision 6506 in 1936 to combat the problem of rain water accumulating in a small pool in the seats. The result was two 9/32-inch holes drilled in the seat in line with the reinforcing washer, which took place in December 1936.

Platform and Citrus Fenders

The parts books indicate that the platform and citrus fenders were altered at serial number 252199. Further changes occurred with tractor 252692, and they were the result of Decision 6122

Model AO was almost identical to Model AR, sharing most of the same dimensions. It is interesting to note that the citrus-type fenders as seen here, although commonly considered an option on the orchard models, were also optional on the basic AR.

The hump in the operator's platform is an easy way to distinguish pre-1937 model AOs. In 1937, the AO-S took the place of the AO, and by the time the AO resumed production in 1941, the hump was gone, as on this tractor.

of February 10, 1936. That decision stated that the rear end of the platform would be raised 2 1/2 inches with the bend in the platform beginning 14 3/8 inches from the rear of the platform. This was done in order to provide more room for the PTO. Also, the toolbox on these tractors was raised 2 3/4 inches.

Carburetor

Deere switched carburetors on these tractors at serial number 252406, the new ones having gray iron bodies instead of the original bronze bodies.

Overdrive Assembly (Special Equipment)

With Decision 6300 of May 12, 1936, Deere & Company announced that a 1:2.75 gear ratio overdrive assembly would be made available as special equipment on the standard-tread As. This decision first affected serial number 252506.

Front-End Eyebolt for Model AO

As a result of Decision 6143, Deere began putting a front-end eyebolt on the front-end support

of Models AO and AI, at serial number 252644. This eyebolt was intended to function as a front-end hitch on these tractors.

Tappet Rods

Tractor 252685 was the first to use the new tappet rods.

Rear Axles

New rear axle shafts were used starting with tractor 253331.

Oil Pump Driveshaft and Heat Indicator

At the beginning of the 1937 model production, just as it had on the row-crop models, the oil pump driveshaft on Model ARs was shortened at serial number 253521. Also occurring at that time were changes to the heat indicator, as recommended by the Stewart-Warner Corporation.

Gearshift Lever

Decision 6563 had two components, affecting Model AR at two different serial numbers. The first change first affected tractor 253796. It swung the end of the gearshift further away from the steering wheel in order to make shifting more convenient; this was accomplished simply by changing the Woodruff key location in the shaft. The second change, which consisted of lengthening the gearshift lever by adding a 1 1/4-inch ball that would serve as a grip on the end of the shaft, occurred on tractor 254202.

Radiator Shutters

Based on Decision 6707, Pines Winterfront Company radiator shutters with guard became regular equipment, beginning with tractor number 253982.

Differential Shaft

Decision 6521 resulted in changes to the differential shaft, first affecting tractor 254055. This involved the removal of 1/16-inch radius from the shaft's short end, along with the addition of a 1 15/32-inch diameter 1/8-inch-wide relief which had a 1/8-inch relief in its bottom.

Skeleton Rear Wheels
(Special Equipment)

In response to demand, Deere approved use of skeleton steel wheels, which had been used on the late GP Wide Tread tractors (with serial numbers 402695 and higher) for the AR as special equipment. This change first affected tractor 254110 in April 1937.

With the "mushroom" covers over the exhaust and air intake, the AO both gave the operator a better forward view and helped reduce the risk of damaging tree limbs with protruding stacks.

TABLE 12A	
Earlier Tractors Using the Drive Wheel and Extension Rim Scrapers	
251454	252179
252072	252181
252110	252188
252144	252189
252145	252193
252149	252196
252169	252197
252170	252198
252173	

Governor Case

As a result of Decision 6877, the radius of the governor case was increased from 7/16 inch to 9/16 inch, starting with tractor 254148.

Front Wheel Weights
(Optional Equipment)

Starting in April 1937, front wheel weights weighing 100 pounds each became available on the AR. These weights, however, could only be used on tractors with spoke wheels (with both steel wheels or rubber tires) and on demountable disc wheels fitted with rubber tires.

The End of the Loop Drawbar

Changes in the drawbar occurring at serial number 254703 were the result of Decision 6853 from March 1937. That decision announced that the original loop drawbars, which Deere called "Drawbar ends having a large forged eye," would be replaced on Models A, AN, AW, and AR by more conventional drawbars. The AR used the new A1821R drawbar, which the decision stated would have a 13/16-inch drilled hole.

Belt Pulley and Other Parts

The fan shaft wasn't the only thing that was updated with tractor 254703. This tractor also featured the new A1864R belt pulley with races, along with a new tappet lever oiler pipe. The belt pulley received a new dust shield at serial number 258155.

Radiator Core

In order to prevent excess water consumption in tractors regularly equipped with radiator shutters, Deere issued Decision 7279, which announced an increase in the size of the radiator core for the A series. The new core used three rows of tubes instead of two, first affecting tractor number 255104.

Magneto and Spark Plug Cables

The AR started using the Edison-Splitdorf Type CD magneto on tractor 255340, toward the end of the 1937 model year. This magneto replaced the Fairbanks-Morse magneto, which had caused a number of complaints from Deere's customers as reported in Decision 7308. This change required new spark plug cables to be used, as well. The right-side cables increased in length from 22 inches to 29 1/2 inches, while the left-side cables increased in length from 27 1/2 inches to 35 1/2 inches.

Radiator Shutters

The radiator shutter assembly on the AR was significantly redesigned as first seen on tractor 255948. This assembly was larger thn its predecessor, thus covering more of the radiator's front.

Cylinder Head

The A587R cylinder head, beginning with tractor 256381, had larger exhaust valve ports (increased in size from 1 5/8 inch to 1 11/16 inch) and other minor changes as a result of Decision 7574 from February 22, 1938.

Oil Pump Driveshaft

Decision 8033 stated that the length of the A1599 oil pump driveshaft on the A series tractors was to be increased from 13 13/16 inches to 13 31/32 inches, and this went into effect at serial number 257004.

Platform and PTO Housing and Guard

Tractor 258330 was the first to use a platform that did not have a hump in the back, which served as a PTO guard. Instead, the new platform was simply flat and a PTO shield was thus necessary. Also, alterations were made to the PTO housing at this time, as well.

Flywheel

Resulting from Decision 8955, the finger grip depressions on the A2237R flywheels were removed and the width of the rim thickness was

As with any steel-wheeled tractor, if you drive it, the lugs are going to lose a lot of paint. While these lugs were originally totally painted, one cannot expect any restored tractor on steel wheels to have immaculate paint on the lugs-that is simply not realistic to any condition, other than the showroom floor.

increased by 1/8 inch. This first affected tractor number 258367.

Oil Filter

Minor changes occurred to the oil filter bottom nut and spring at serial numbers 258000 and 258890.

Steering Wheel

A new French & Hecht three-spoke steering wheel was used on AR 259276. The result of Decision 8935, the new steering wheel featured a

These three tractors have their hood decals in three different locations. Indeed, the location of those stencils changed frequently on tractors that left the factory. A good general rule to make your tractor as close to "correct" as possible with regard to hood decal placement is to either take good notes and pictures of where the decals originally were on your tractor, or, if you can't tell, simply try to place the decals as close to the center of the hood sides as possible.

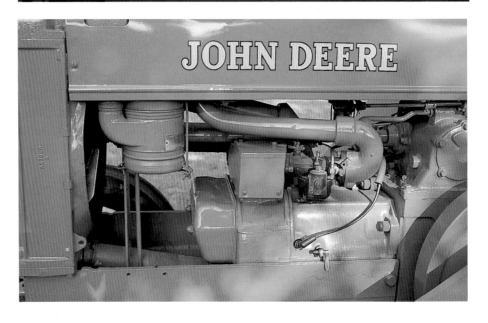

round steel hub with pressed-in spokes, whereas the previous steering wheel had had a cast center with riveted-in spokes.

High-Speed Transmissions

Deere & Company issued Decisions 9147 and 9148 on March 18, 1940, approving special high-speed transmissions for these tractors that provided top speeds of 13 miles per hour and 11.5 miles per hour, respectively. The latter decision was made to "meet speeds required for AO Tractors in Florida."

Major Changes for 1941

The beginning of 1941 production for the standard-tread ARs commenced with serial number 260000; Deere scrapped a number of serial numbers preceding it. The 1941 models AR and AO sported many new features as outlined here.

Engine Components

Over one year after Deere decided to increase the engine size of its row-crop A tractors, the company published Decision 9250 to incorporate those changes into its standard-tread As. That decision, published in October 1940, went into effect right on schedule with AR 260000 on November 15, 1940.

The changes caused by this decision were extensive. For one, the new A2324R cylinder block replaced the A732R block. These tractors also boasted different crankshafts, flywheels, connecting rods, pistons, piston pins, and related items. Additionally, the A2325R cylinder head supplanted the original A587R head, thus requiring new valves, valve guides, and exhaust valve springs. Also necessary were a new manifold, manifold studs, tappet levers with shaft, and a tappet cover. The spark plugs were also changed, though Champion, AC, and Auto-Lite brand plugs were still in use.

Carburetor

A new carburetor body was used, featuring improved nozzles and other components, which required the use of a new air cleaner inlet pipe.

Transmission, PTO, and Rear End

To work sufficiently with the im-proved engine, the standard-tread A's transmission also underwent improvements. These transmission improvements included a new countershaft with a new housing, gear, cone, spacers, washers, idler gear, and other parts; a redesigned overdrive gear shaft and gear with gear-shifter handle; sliding

Top and bottom: One must be careful when buying reproduction sheet metal or when repairing the sheet metal on his or her tractor. Unique features of the sheet metal need to be maintained in order for a restoration to be correct to original manufacture.

This 1936 Model AR has the hump at the rear of the operator's platform. This is a quick way to distinguish earlier models from later ones, and one should note this change when considering buying a parts tractor.

gear pinion; and improved high- and low-speed gear assemblies.

Deere installed redesigned PTO components in these tractors as well. First, the original PTO shaft (which measured 1 7/16 x 33 3/4 inches) was replaced by a shorter shaft that measured only 1 1/2 x 28 1/2 inches. Additional changes affected the rear PTO housing, bevel gears, shifter shaft, shifter, and other parts. Also needed was a different PTO power shaft sliding gear.

The differential was improved, featuring a new differential shaft and bearing cones and cups. Furthermore, new final drives were used, as was a new rear axle housing cover.

Main Case and Oil Pump Body

With the new engine and transmission came revisions to the main case. That, in turn, required changes to the oil pump body casting. These new parts were the result of moving the oil pump to a more effective location near the bottom of the crankcase.

Cooling System Components

These tractors also sported revised cooling systems, which included a new radiator core. Accompanying the new core were new radiator

A good restoration should look nice from a distance as well as up close, though in most instances one cannot determine if all the parts on a tractor are correct without close inspection.

sides; radiator bottom tank with lower water pipe, inlet, and hose; radiator top tank with upper water pipe, inlet, and hose. Also, a new round radiator cap supplanted the original oblong cast cap.

With all the changes that the radiator underwent, a redesign of the entire radiator shutter assembly was also required. Unfortunately, specific dimensions of these changes are unavailable, but the size of the new shutters corresponded with that of the new radiator.

Wheels and Tires

AR 260000 was the first tractor to be affected by yet another decision: it was the first AR to be equipped with all-rubber tires as standard equipment. According to Decision 9560 of October 1940, this change in standard equipment was made since about 53 percent of the standard-tread As which Deere had sold since July 1, 1939, had been equipped with all-rubber tires. By virtue of this decision, 11.25x24 four-ply rear tires and 6.00x16 four-ply front tires were made standard on all standard-tread As, including the AR. However, 26-inch tires were actually made standard.

Headlights

Tractor 260000 was the first to offer 5-inch headlights instead of the 7-inch lights that were previously offered.

Other Changes at Serial Number 260000

Other items that were either improved or new to the AR and AO at this point were the three-way fuel cock, crankcase, and ventilator pipe.

Changes Made to the Model AO Only

The Model AO underwent changes that affected only it at this time, as well. In improving the brakes, the brake housings, shafts, and latches were updated. Additionally, the AO received updates to its steering components, including a new rear steering shaft support and a steering worm with housing.

The Changes Continue

Upholstered Seat (Special Equipment)

Deere approved use of the upholstered seat on the Model AR on June 13, 1941, with Decision 9937.

Heat Indicator and PTO Shaft

Even though the heat indicator seems to have been changed at serial number 262700, it appears that Deere reverted back to the original with

The front-end eyebolt is an easy way to distinguish the later ARs and AOs from the earlier units.

tractor 264300. The PTO shaft was lengthened and strengthened at serial number 262700, the new dimensions being 1 3/8 inch by 30 1/16 inch.

Main Bearings

The main bearings underwent changes at serial numbers 263031 and 263500, according to the parts books.

Fan Shaft

Tractor 264644 was the first to have its fan shaft shortened by 1/8 inch over the previous dimensions. The new shaft measured 38 3/8 inches in length.

Camshaft

The A3583R camshaft replaced the A1142R shaft at tractor number 270616. Also affected by that change were the camshaft housing and bearing cones and cups.

The early unstyled ARs and AOs should have the Leaping Deer stencil on the back of the gasoline-starting tank as it appears on these two tractors. Also, the magneto should not be painted; the cover should be black.

Paint and Decals

Like most A series tractors, the unstyled AR and AO are typically painted John Deere green with John Deere yellow wheels and lettering. As for cast-in letters and numbers, only those appearing on the "JOHN DEERE" on the radiator top tank were painted yellow; all other letters and part numbers remained John Deere green. Spark plugs, spark plug wires, the magneto, petcocks, and the steering wheel grip all remained in their original color. All gauge faces and light lenses were covered, as were tires, when painting occurred. The light casings were painted black. Though wheel hub center colors varied, the front hubs were almost always painted yellow, as were any nuts used on both the front and rear wheels.

For most of these tractors, the leaping deer trademark decal appeared on the gasoline-starting tank. The exact location of the "JOHN DEERE" decal/stencil on the hood sides varied

tremendously, though the most predominant position is such that the top and bottom are equidistant from the top and bottom of the hood sides and similarly, with the ends of the de-cals equidistant from the ends of the hood.

Apart from the generally accepted rules, there were a few changes that were made over the years:

Hood Stencil

Decision 5807 of September 28, 1935, announced that the D2395 stencil should be used on both sides of the hood. This was to take effect around November 12, 1935.

Model Designation on Rear Axle Housing Cover

Also resulting from Decision 5807 (and to take place at the same time), the "MODEL AR" and "MODEL AO" stencils were to appear on the rear axle housings of those respective tractors.

Patent Transfers

Alterations were to be made to the A826 patent transfer, consisting of the addition of numbers 1,867,582; 2,037,083; and 2,102,543 as outlined in Decision 7548. This went into effect on tractor 257000 on August 1, 1939.

While no documents were found regarding decals on the AR and AO, it is possible that by the time this tractor—a 1944 model—was produced, the decal on the back of the gasoline-starting tank had been changed to the one seen here. Indeed, the original decal found in this location was out of use on the row-crop models by the time this 1944 tractor was built.

Highway Yellow

Deere approved the use of Highway Yellow paint on the Model AR with Decision 9937 from June 1941. This was the result of the AI's termination.

Leaping Deer Trademark Transfer

Decision 9896 stated that Deere would "adopt decalcomania transfer to replace the Leaping Deer trade mark now plaster branded on our product." The new JD122 Leaping Deer transfer would measure 4 inches, and it started use on July 14, 1941.

Patent Transfers

Issued on May 9, 1941, Decision 9911 announced that the borders on the A826R patent transfers, used on Models AR and AO, would be changed from red to black. This decision was to be made effective on or before Valentine's Day 1944.

Many parts that were common between the standard-tread As and the row-crop As were changed on both model types at roughly the same point in time.

Whether simply the standard-tread AR or the orchard-friendly AO, all of the standard-tread versions of the Model A were very well suited for the jobs Deere designed them to perform.

Chapter 7

The Model AO-S

Deere initiated a series of decisions to redesign the already existing AO as a result of responding to the need for a specialized standard-tread A for use in orchards. Today, this model is known as the "AO-S," or the "AO Streamlined." Both of those designations appear in Deere advertising literature. However, most of Deere's decisions regarding this model simply referred to it as the "1937 Model 'AO' Tractor."

The AO-S had a number of advantages over the regular AO, which resulted from the more compact size of the tractor. By using the front-end setup and drag links of the Model AI, the AO-S had only a 68 3/4-inch wheelbase when compared to the AO's 75 3/4-inch wheelbase. Additionally, the AO-S was only 124 1/4 inches long. The short wheelbase of the AO-S made a shorter turning radius possible—an important benefit, particularly for orchard work. Coupled with responsive steering and individual rear wheel brakes, the AO-S could change direction inside a 9-foot turning radius.

The 1937 Model AO was also narrower than the earlier AO. Overall, the AO-S was 5 1/4 inches narrower than the AO when equipped with either steel wheels or rubber tires. The brunt of the width reductions came from the new shorter rear axle housings, reducing tread width from 50 5/8 inches to only 45 3/8 inches accounting for the 5 1/4-inch difference. Deere also changed the front axle, crankshaft, and clutch assembly. The belt pulley, which

stayed at the same diameter, had its face shortened from 7 inches to 6 1/4 inches. And, despite the changes to the engine, it did retain the 5 1/2x6 1/2-inch bore and stroke, just like all of the other A series tractors.

The AO-S was also shorter than its predecessor; its total height was cut from 58 1/2 inches to 53 1/8 inches. Deere accomplished that feat by redesigning the hood, fuel tank, radiator and radiator cap, and even the steering gear. At the front of the tractor, the radiator cap sat only 52 1/4 inches above the ground. The fenders of the AO-S were also redesigned, being 50 1/4 inches high at the highest point instead of the 51 inches of the AO. Additionally, the AO-S had a shorter steering post that set the steering shaft at a 12-degree angle, leaving the top of the steering wheel below the cowl line. Accordingly, the seat of the tractor was also lowered from 38 1/2 inches to 34 7/8 inches. All of these changes contributed to making the AO-S better suited for orchard work by reducing the chances of fruit or limbs being damaged.

Of all the differences between the AO-S and the AO, however, perhaps none are more apparent than the differences in styling. The most

Introduced in the 1937 model year, the Model AO-S was, indeed, one of the most streamlined tractors of its time. It was certainly the most stylish-looking standard-tread Model A, and its production is interesting, since Deere did not stylize the Models AO and AR until the 1950 model year.

Produced along with the unstyled row-crop As, the AO-S used a similar decal style and arrangement, though the words "General Purpose" were not included on the hood decal.

dashing feature of the streamlined model was the "V"-type radiator screen, which resembled a snow plow. The AO Streamlined also had a new hood with improved pulley and flywheel guards. Furthermore, it had a cowl and full crown fenders. These features all were intended to protect the trees and the fruit.

Yet another AO-S feature was the redesigned drawbar and support. The pivot point for drawbar was moved forward, from 7 3/4 inches in front of the rear axle center line to 14 inches in front of it. These changes were supposedly made to allow better performance with the orchard disc.

Futuristic-looking with its sleek fenders and pointed grille screen, the AO Streamlined boasted a few styling concepts that were used on the upcoming 1939 styled A row-crops. The AO-S was the first A series tractor to use grille screens, and it was also the first to use a "JOHN DEERE" medallion-type stencil/transfer on the nose of the tractor. Interestingly, Deere literature on the AO-S shows that medallion to be of a smaller size than the one found on this tractor.

Deere & Company certainly did not ignore the operator when designing the AO-S. Not only did the operator's low position help protect the trees, but it also made the operator's work less prone to injuries.

One of the things that made the AO-S so well suited for orchard work was its low, compact design. As evident here, the top of the tractor was almost totally flat, thus reducing the overall height of the tractor.

Deere didn't ignore operator conveniences in the new AO-S, either. Despite having a smaller platform as a result of the narrowed space between the rear wheels, the operator was not cramped. A more comfortable seat, protection from tree limbs, and a nice dashboard—a novelty for tractors of that era—made operation of this model easier. A change in the brakes required an easier-to-operate brake pedal location over the top of the rear axle housing.

One problem that the styling of the AO-S caused was that of starting the tractor. While the tractor looked futuristic, it still had the conventional hand-start feature. Furthermore, the hand starting was done via turning the flywheel in what Deere referred to as an "anticlockwise" direction; and that flywheel just happened to be located *beneath* the new stylish covers of the tractor.

Changes

Here are some of the more notable changes that the AO-S endured.

Differential Shaft

Changes to the AO-S's A485 differential shaft first occurred on AO 1031. This change was identical to that made to the Model AR's differential shaft at serial number 254055 as discussed in chapter 6.

Sheet Metal

On March 31, 1937, Deere's Decision 6869 initiated a number of changes to the Streamlined AO's sheet metal. The extensive changes—first evident retroactively on AO 1045 of mid-February 1937—affected the AA-1345 cowl assembly, the AA-1340 dash and toolbox assembly, and the AA-1328 hood assembly. Beginning at the same time, citrus fenders appeared as an option resulting from Decision 6550.

Decision 6887 of April 5, 1937, made provisions for many additional minor changes to the tractors' fenders, pulley guards, and flywheel guards. These changes were first seen in July of that year.

Most of the general rules of two-cylinder John Deere tractor painting and decal placement also apply to the AO Streamlined. Thus, these tractors were largely green with yellow wheels. Even the grille screens were supposed to be green, not the trim color (in this case yellow), which is the norm for other manufacturers' tractors.

Gearshift Lever

One of the earliest changes to the AO-S's gearshift was rather minor. In order to make shifting easier, Deere changed the location of the Woodruff key. This necessitated relocating the gearshift lever further down, away from the steering wheel. This was first done with tractor 1123. With AO-S 1338, the gearshift lever was lengthened and a 1 1/4-inch-diameter ball was added to the end of the lever to act as a grip.

TABLE 13
Tractors Affected by Decision 6939 of April 20, 1937
1320
1327
1329 to 1335
1337 to 1340

Also true for the sleek AO Streamlined are the normal rules applying to paint (or lack thereof) for the spark plug wires, spark plugs, petcocks, magneto, and gauges.

What tree limb wouldn't flow over the contoured lines of the Model AO-S? While most orchard tractors of this era had sheet metal designed such that it forced the limbs over the tires and similar obstructions, the AO-S's sheet metal simply let the limbs glide over the tractor, almost as if by their own volition.

Located near the flywheel, the data plates on the Model AO Streamlined-just as with the data plate on almost any A series tractor-should be masked off before one paints the tractor.

Control Linkage

In May 1937, the shutter control rod (A-1797) on these tractors was reduced in length from 78 7/16 inches to only 78 inches.

Toolbox

Based on Decision 6939, a new expanded metal bottom was used in the AO-S toolboxes, beginning with tractor 1344 on July 27, 1937. This toolbox, which was also used on the following AO-Ss, was used in order to reduce dust and trash buildup.

Hubcap

AO 1389 was the first to receive the newly renovated special equipment A1555R front hubcap.

TABLE 14
Earlier Tractors Affected by Decisions 6952 and 6984 of May 7, 1937

1319	1439
1321	1440
1429	1442
1433	1443
1435	1446
1438	

While no documents were found regarding the paint guidelines for this model, it is entirely possible (and probably likely) that both the air intake and exhaust openings were painted green or at least affected by overspray.

Its depth was increased 3/16 inch over the previous hubcap, and the height of its bolting pads was increased about 1/2 inch.

Drawbar

Deere strengthened the drawbar of this model by increasing its thickness from 3/4 inch to 7/8 inch. This resulted from Decision 7098, which went into effect on tractor 1425. This feature was also applied to earlier AO Streamlineds with serial numbers 1320, 1338, 1343, 1379, 1381, 1382, 1408, and 1419.

Dash and Citrus Fenders

Publishing Decision 6952 on May 7, 1937, Deere decided to add a hinged opening on the

While finding a Model AO-S is challenging enough, correct restoration of one of these tractors can be a nightmare. Not only are paint records hard to locate, but this rare model underwent many changes in its short production span, meaning that very few tractors are the same.

pulley side guard of the AO Streamlined's citrus fenders; this new opening would be similar to the one already present on the flywheel side, and its purpose was the same: ease of access. This constituted the use of additional braces in that area. Deere also decided to use more ribs and braces in the fender over the rear wheel to prevent excess vibration. In addition, to accommodate the larger 12.75x24-inch oversize rear tires, the fenders were widened by 1 inch on each side. At the same time, by virtue of Decision 6984, the AO-S's dash reinforcing strip (A-1714) was shortened by 3/8 inch. All of these changes first went into effect on August 4, 1937 on tractor 1447, although earlier serial numbers tractors were also affected.

Paint and Decals

The AO-S was also typically John Deere green with John Deere yellow wheels. By virtue of Decision 6685, this model was to sport the A1780 hood stencil on both sides of the hood and the A1064 leaping deer trademark stencil on the dash from the start of production.

Chapter 8

The Model AI

The first John Deere–designed letter series tractor was the Model D, introduced in 1923, some 11 years before the A's introduction. The D was a very popular tractor, and by the mid-1920s Deere decided to expand its markets by selling the D as an industrial tractor—the Model DI. Deere also cooperated with the Hawkeye Maintainer Company of Waterloo, Iowa, to fit a special version of the D with a Hawkeye road maintainer, a project that only lasted from the 1929 to 1931 production years. Both of these attempts to establish Deere in the industrial market were unsuccessful, but Deere was not down for the count. In 1936, the company made a decisive move to break into the industrial market.

The impetus was Deere's Decision 6100 of February 15, 1936. It announced Deere's adoption of the Model AI, an industrial version of the Model A. Basically a derivative of the Model AR, the AI was to be painted Industrial Yellow and sport black stenciled lettering.

Deere knew that industrial tractors had to be more than just regular agricultural tractors painted yellow, though. For starters, the company acknowledged that industrial tractors were often used in tight quarters, thus good maneuverability was desirable in those units. To accommodate

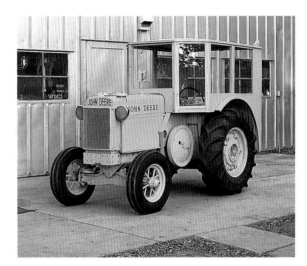

Here is the very first Model AI, serial number 252334. This tractor bears many of the features introduced by Decision 6100, which announced the AI, and other preproduction decisions.

The AI sported the special air-intake and exhaust covers that resembled mushrooms. These covers, like those used on the orchard tractors, helped give the operator a less obstructed forward view and made the AI more adaptable to use with front-mounted machinery.

Deere's Model AI started production in 1936, with production ceasing five years later. This standard-tread tractor derived from the Model AR was well suited for industrial applications and could be fitted with a wide variety of special equipment.

Important in determining if an AI is correct to original manufacture is whether it has the original-style front axle. While regular AR-type front axles could be fitted, the AI came with a special front axle that featured bosses and notches. The AI's front axle was positioned farther back than on the AR, as well, making the tractor shorter-coupled and more maneuverable.

Restoring the first tractor in any series can be particularly challenging, as these tractors are different from anything that came before. And, indeed, they often are different from anything that came after them in at least some respects. Referring to historical documents won't always answer all of your questions correctly. No matter if the tractor you are restoring is the first or in the middle of a production run, historical documents are a place to start.

Based on its serial number, this AI is supposed to have the special side-mounted seat according to Deere documents. In some cases this option would not be correct on tractors produced before serial number 253141, but Deere did outfit some earlier tractors with this option.

this, Decision 6100 announced that the AI would have a 7-inch-shorter wheelbase than did its agricultural counterpart—the AR—shortening it from 76 to 69 inches. This change required the use of a shorter radius rod and drag link. The resultant production AI had a turning radius of 12 feet 8 inches, down from the AR's 13-foot turning radius.

But Deere had other reasons for moving the front axle back other than just to improve maneuverability. That new placement also allowed front-mounted industrial equipment to be located closer to the tractor's radiator, thereby improving the balance of the tractor. Had the heavy industrial equipment been mounted farther in front of the tractor, more downward force would have been applied to the front axle, making turning more difficult. Also, by having the industrial equipment mounted closer to the radiator, more of the tractor's weight would be applied to the rear wheels, thus increasing traction. Other characteristics of the AI that permitted the mounting of industrial equipment on its front end were the finished pads and tapped holes on the front axle.

Yet another change that Deere deemed necessary was the strengthening of the drawbar on the AI. This drawbar had a vertical adjustment from 12 3/4 inches to 14 inches from the ground.

All of the items included in Decision 6100 were to go into effect on March 15, 1936. The decision actually went into effect on AI 252334 on March 18, 1936. Deere apparently did not give the AI its own separate serial number run, interspersing these industrial tractors with the AR and AO serial numbers.

Preproduction Changes

Prior to the start of AI production in the spring of 1936, Deere published a number of other decisions regarding the upcoming model. Most of those decisions were scheduled to become effective with Decision 6100, and many were first realized on that first AI, tractor 252334.

The first decision announcing preproduction changes was Decision 6127, dated February 8, 1936. It made individual hand-operated rear wheel brakes available as optional equipment for the AI. On April 3, 1936, AI 252346 became the first AI to take advantage of that feature.

Five days after publishing Decision 6127, Deere announced in Decision 6129 that two different high-pressure tire and wheel assemblies—AA-1053 and AA-1061—would be made optional for the AI. The first consisted of 9 x 24-inch single rear tires and 6 x 16-inch front tires. With this

The restoration of this AI appears to be nearly perfect in terms of originality. However, closer inspection is necessary to determine if the hood decals are the correct 3-inch-tall variety. The wheel and tire combination on this tractor also appears to be original.

arrangement, the AI would have a rear tread of 51 1/2 inches, a front tread of 47 inches, and an overall width of 61 inches. The second package would have virtually the same tires but would have duals on the rear. That widened the unit to 81 3/4 inches. The AA-1061 package was first used on AI 252380 on March 9, 1937, while the AA-1053 setup was first used on AI 254346 on May 7, 1937.

In order to provide yet another front-end hitch point for Models AI, AO, BR, and BO, Deere published Decision 6143 on February 21, 1936. This new hitch was simply an eyebolt A1297, which was screwed into the front axle. This decision went into effect in late April 1936 on the AI and AO.

Since industrial tractors also saw heavy work in less-than-desirable conditions, outside-mounted valve stems were often in danger of being damaged. Thus, Deere deemed it necessary to move the valve stems on the AA-869 and AD-1379 front wheels of the AI and DI to the inside of the wheels. This became reality on those tractors around May 1936, and Deere made this feature optional on Models AR, AO, and D.

Rear wheel weights became available on the AI in the summer of 1936, so any tractor produced after that time would be correct with this feature. The very early AIs, however, would not be correct if restored with rear wheel weights.

The side power shaft is an extremely rare option on the Model AI, usually found on tractors equipped with the Hyster Hoists and LaPlant-Choate cranes, which required this feature for operation. But the first AIs produced did not have either the side power shaft or those mounted pieces of equipment as options. This tractor, serial number 257175, was produced late enough that those options would be correct.

Deere approved the use of LaPlant-Choate cranes late in 1937, so these unique additions should not be found on most 1937 or earlier tractors. This crane was the right power for an AI; if such a crane lifted much more than its capacity, there was a tendency for the tractors to flip.

Published just one day before it reportedly went into effect on AI 252334, Decision 6206 stated that both the air stack cap support and exhaust opening cover support would be increased in diameter from 6 3/4 inches to 6 7/8 inches. This also affected the Model AO and was to be an option on the AR.

Decision 6280 was not exactly a preproduction decision (it was published in late April 1936), but it seems that Decision 6280 was retroactive since the first AI was affected by it. This decision stated that in order to reduce problems in manufacturing, the AA-897 transmission brake cover was to be changed in shape from polygonal to cylindrical.

Optional and Special Equipment

After production's inception, additional optional and special equipment became available on the AI.

Low-Pressure Rear Tires

In late April 1936, Deere approved the use of 12.75x24-inch low-pressure tires on the Model AI as special equipment. Even though this decision was to go into effect immediately, it seems that it was not put into effect until much later in September 1938.

Overdrive Assembly

The 1:2.75 overdrive gear ratio assembly, which had previously been available on the row-crop As, became available on the standard-tread As by virtue of Decision 6300 of May 12, 1936. This overdrive assembly increased the speeds of the AI quite a bit. According to this decision, the new assembly caused a 1.33-mile-per-hour increase in speed in third gear and a 2.09-mile-per-hour increase in speed in fourth gear on, AIs with standard wheel equipment. Similarly, on tractors with the optional 12.75x24-inch low-pressure rear tires, the use of this overdrive resulted in a 1.35-mile-per-hour increase in speed in third gear and a 2.11-mile-per-hour increase in fourth gear.

Rear Wheel Weights

Deere made rear wheel weights available in mid-May 1936. These weights could only be mounted on the outside of the rear wheels.

Side Power Shaft and Hyster Hoists

With Decision 6324 of May 29, 1936, Deere approved the use of two Williamette-Hyster Company front-mounted hoists on the AI. The approved hoists were the Model JD-AD Double Drum Hyster and the Model JD-AS Single Drum Hyster. Interestingly, these were to be used on AIs equipped with side power shafts, an option that had not yet been outlined by Deere's decisions. That decision, number 6327, came on June 3, 1936.

The new special-equipment side power shaft was mounted in the tractors' modified first reduction gear cover. According to Decision 6327, the power shaft measured 1.374–1.375 inches in diameter and was 1 13/16 inches long. The shaft also had a provision for a 5/16-inch square key and a 3/4-inch 16 NF slotted nut. When the engine of the AI operated at 975 rpm, the power shaft turned at 763 rpm (according to a later decision). In addition to being used on a few AIs, this special assembly also saw use on A 440110 and AR 253110.

Special Seat Mount

When drawn, road maintaining equipment trailed the AI, it was sometimes awkward for the tractor operator to control the equipment. Therefore, Deere announced on June 23, 1936, that a special sidewise-mounted seat would be available for both the AI and BI. AIs fitted with this feature are listed on Table 15.

Solid Rubber Tires

Deere authorized use of solid rubber tires on this model in July 1936. These front wheels measured 24 x 3 1/2 inches, decreasing the front tread from 47 1/8 inches to only 45 5/8 inches. Two different solid-rubber-tired rear wheels were

available, as well. The new 40 x 5-inch wheels with solid rubber tires decreased the rear wheel tread from 52 inches to 49 1/8 inches and shortened the overall width of the tractor from 64 to only 55 inches. Also optional were larger 40 x 8-inch rear wheels with solid rubber tires, which provided a rear tread of 50 1/8 inches and a 59-inch overall width.

Automatic Coupler and Pintle Hook Assembly

To better suit industrial demands, Deere made these items—which were painted Highway Yellow—available with Decision 6388 of July 23, 1936. According to Deere documents,

The yellow used on the industrial tractors is not the same as regular John Deere yellow. Thus, restorers need to make sure they are using the proper paint when restoring these tractors.

Enthusiasts should not restore an early AI such as this 1936 model with the incorrect lighting system if they want to remain correct to original manufacture. Although early AIs could come with the optional K.W. lighting system, Deere eliminated the system later in production due to problems.

Even when fitted with the optional equipment, most AIs should still conform to the general rules of yellow paint and black stenciled-on letters. These details can be hard to spot when hidden beneath mounted equipment, however.

The AI was a durable tractor, but these units often were used in harsh conditions and may prove more challenging to restore than their agricultural counterparts.

Though stenciling was the rule for the AI, many collectors resort to using the much more convenient and less messy decals. The hood decals should appear in basically the same location as they appear on the Model AR, for example-centered on the hood.

The AI could be fitted with a variety of optional equipment, thus making this model one of the more interesting to restore.

TABLE 15
Als Using the Side-Wise Seat Mount

252334	252477
252358	252723
252380	252731
252381	252737
252382	252740
252415	252749
252425	252759
252434	252799
252435	252925
252436	252926
252453	253004
252455	253016
252475	253140
252476	

neither of these items found their home on an AI until September of that year.

Front Wheel Odometer

Deere & Company approved use of "Habodometer" odometers as manufactured by Veeder Root, Inc. of Hartford, Connecticut, on the AI tractors. According to Decision 6733, this was put in effect on February 1, 1937, the same day the decision was published.

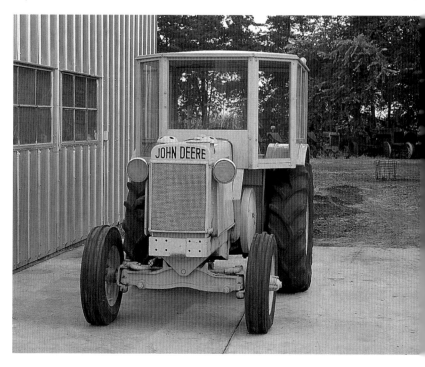

Just as the letters on the radiator top tank of Models AR and AO appear in yellow, the letters on the AI's radiator top tank should be painted black to correspond with the decals.

When painting a Model AI, it is advisable to mask off items such as the magneto (or distributor), wires, and gauges, as those items should not appear in yellow. When painting the gauge casings black, it is best to mask off the gauge faces as well.

Front Wheel Weights

These weights, weighing in at 100 pounds, could be fitted on any A with spoke wheels or demountable disc wheels. Decision 6894 of April 1937 announced the availability of these weights as special equipment on those tractors, and it was put into effect later that month.

Battery and Generator Electric Lighting

In mid-September 1937, Deere & Company published a decision announcing an electric lighting system that would prove more useful for the AI than the K.W. system used at the time. The new system, complete with an automotive-type battery and generator plus a light switch, could be used even if the tractor was not running. This change went into effect sometime around October 1937.

Centrifugal Pump

Decision 7329, dated October 5, 1937, approved immediate usage of the Model B-LFK, Type P, Sterling Centrifugal Pump on the AI. When fitted with this pump, which had a 700-gallon-per-minute capacity, AIs had to use Deere's AD-456 solid-rubber-tired wheels.

Crane

On October 18, 1937, Deere authorized for the AI immediate usage of the Model CA crane as produced by the LaPlant-Choate Manufacturing Company, Inc., of Cedar Rapids, Iowa. In order to use this crane, AIs had to be equipped with the side power shaft. Deere advertising literature proclaimed that the LaPlant-Choate crane used on the AI could, depending on the wheel equipment of the tractor, handle loads between 2,700 and 3,400 pounds with the boom retracted. Extension of the boom only reduced handling capacity 1,700 to 2,300 pounds for the AI.

Street Flusher and Sprinkler

Effective on May 1, 1938, Deere approved the use of its Street Flusher and Sweeper for the Model AI.

A number of moving parts on AIs were once painted, but they often lost that paint during operation. Those parts include the clutch pulley, and, on this AI, chains and gears used to power mounted implements. Since this wear is associated with operation, a tractor is still correct to original manufacture even if some of the paint is missing from those areas.

The Model AI is one of the most noticeable versions of the Model A, and it remains quite popular with collectors today.

Snow Plow

As a result of Decision 9097 of February 1940, AIs equipped with 6.5 x 16-inch six-ply front tires could be fitted with two different "SNO-FLYR" snow plows, Models EH and EHW. The Wm. Bros. Boiler and Manufacturing Co. of Minneapolis, Minnesota, produced those plows.

Changes

Most of the changes that took place on Models AR and AO also took place on the AI at the same time. Please refer to chapter 6 to see a list of the changes made to the standard-tread tractors.

Paint and Decals

Most AIs were simply Highway Yellow with black stenciled-on lettering, a standard established by Decision 6100, which announced the AI. However, Deere did later make it possible for AIs to sport different paint schemes. Decision 7129 of June 29, 1937, which allowed varying paint schemes, was issued to comply with var-

ious states' laws and city ordinances. The available colors were light red, gray, blue, orange, green, and a yellow other than the standard AI Highway Yellow.

Originally, Deere applied a "JOHN DEERE" stencil composed of 3-inch letters on the side of the hood. Decision 9859 of April 1941 dictated a new lettering style. The new letters were only 2 1/2 inches tall. This decision went into effect on March 24, 1942.

The AI's Demise

Due to a lack of customer demand, Deere decided to discontinue its line of industrial tractors—including Models AI, BI, and DI—as of July 1, 1941, by virtue of Decision 9900. As a result of that decision, Deere almost instantly made upholstered seats and Highway Yellow paint schemes available on the agricultural versions of those tractors in order to meet any future demand for industrial-type tractors.

Chapter 9

The Styled Models AR and AO

Perhaps the primary reason why the standard-tread versions of the Model A remained unstyled for as long as they did was that it took money to effect change. Deere probably didn't think that sales of the AR and AO were high enough to warrant making such changes. By 1949, however, Deere had changed its stance.

The row-crop versions of most of Deere's row-crop tractors had been styled since 1939; those tractor models had again been updated drastically both stylistically and mechanically for the 1947 model year. By that time the standard-tread Model D had been styled for years, and sales of that model far surpassed that of the standard-tread AR. Excellent sales figures were certainly a result of more than just the appearance of the tractors, but styling undoubtedly did influence some farmers' decisions regarding which tractor to buy.

As early as the mid-1930s, Deere began experimenting with a tractor that was originally intended to replace the Model D. Deere decided to power the new design with diesel fuel. Diesel was a new concept to Deere and relatively new to the wheel tractor market. That experimental model evolved into the Model R, which Deere

released for the 1949 model year. The R, however, did not replace the D as originally planned.

What the R did do, however, was give the standard-tread Deeres an entirely new look. The D had been Deere's only stylized standard-tread tractor, featuring vertical slats on the grille screens. The R did away with those slats, though, and the result was an even tougher-appearing tractor.

While the styled AR did look a lot like the R, the two tractors were quite different. Most significantly, the R was strictly a diesel-powered tractor, but the AR was not available with that fuel type.

Models AR and AO were finally styled for the 1950 model year, and they took their look from the standard-tread, diesel-powered Model R, which Deere had recently introduced. Thus, the styled AR became known to many as "Baby R."

The change in styling for the AR and AO was actually more stunning than those changes Deere had made to the row-crop models for 1939. In addition to being different-looking, the new AR was also bigger, due in part to its larger engine.

So, when Deere introduced the styled version of the Model AR, it is not surprising that the basic styling design that was used on the R was implemented on the AR. The styled Model AR, in fact, looked so similar to the Model R that it acquired the nickname "Baby R." Production of the styled Model AR began in early June 1949, and those early tractors were included in the 1950 model year production.

The new Model AR was vastly different from the unstyled version it replaced. The styling alone contributed to a number of changes, many of which concerned operator comfort. One of the most noticeable changes from the operator's perspective was the new, padded seat with backrest. Much like the seat that Deere placed on the A as standard equipment beginning in the 1947 model year, the AR's new seat could be adjusted both forward and backward to suit the operator's desire. The AR was brought up to par with the row-crop tractors in terms of mechanical features, as well.

A number of changes also served to improve the operator's view. For one, the seat was offset to the right such that the operator could look down the side of the tractor better than he or she could have had the seat been centered. Additionally, the styled AR incorporated the intake and exhaust stack arrangement (with the exhaust stack directly in front of the air intake stack), which Deere had been using on the row-crop As since 1939. The stack arrangement was changed for the same reason it was changed on the row-crop tractors: to cut down on the obstructions to the operator's view.

This model came standard with a PTO, distributor ignition complete with battery and starter, two fender-mounted headlights, combination rear light with red warning lamp, belt pulley, swinging drawbar, muffler, and spark arrester.

The Changes Begin
Clutch and Fan Changes
Serial number 273080 marked the beginning of the use of an almost entirely new clutch assembly. Also altered at this time was the air intake stack and bracket. Other changes affected the fan bearing housing with tube and certain related parts.

PTO Shifter Arm

Tractor 273492 was the first to use a new PTO shifter arm.

PTO

Deere made changes to the PTO shaft with tractor 274681, the new A4566R shaft appearing.

Transmission

A number of changes took place in the transmission of the standard-tread As, beginning at serial number 274749. Parts involved included the first reduction gear, the drive gear for the sliding gear shaft, and other related small parts. Then, at serial number 275338, the right-hand-side sliding gear shaft cover was changed.

Throttle Rod

Deere made an alteration in the throttle control rod and end with tractor 275412 by changing it to the swivel type.

Distributor and New Coil

Prior to tractor 275533, the AR and AO used a Wico distributor. The newer tractors, however, used a Delco-Remy distributor and coil.

Generator Field Coil

A new generator field coil and accompanying pole shoe and insulator were first installed on these tractors at serial number 276082.

Crank End Seal and Tappet Lever Shaft

The seal located between the flywheel and the crank changed from cork to rubber at number 276578. Deere also began using a new tappet lever shaft at the same time.

Rear Light

The AR and AO started using a new rear combination lamp and warning light along with accompanying mounting bracket and related parts at serial number 276780.

From the front, the new AR had a more stylish grille with a hood medallion. From the side, the new tractor had an entirely different hood setup, with different hood decals and a new "AR-in-Circle" decal on the grille sides. From the rear, the styled AR featured clamshell fenders, a battery box seat, a totally redesigned platform, and in-line exhaust and air intake stacks for better forward vision.

The placement of the "AR-in-Circle" decal on this AR is just about right. This is the general area where the decal shows up on period advertising literature and other sources.

From the operator's perspective, the AR did not provide a very good forward view, at least not up close. However, such a view was not critical on these tractors, although it was critical on the row-crop tractors.

Generator Drive Pulley

Deere started using a new generator drive pulley on the standard-tread As beginning with tractor 277177.

Petcocks

Serial number 278150 marked a change in the AR and AO tractors' petcocks. The new part was A4242R, while the older petcocks were AB1898R.

Governor Case

A change in the governor case occurred at serial number 278197. Later changes affected tractor 279532 with the new part A3832R. It was later replaced by the A3267R case at serial number 279532.

Oil Filler Nipple

Slight changes to the oil filler nipple first affected tractor 278843, the 29H398R nipple was supplanted by the A4234R nipple.

The AR was made to work, and that field in the background was its office. No tractor had absolutely perfect paint on it when it left the factory, so tractors today shouldn't be held to that standard either.

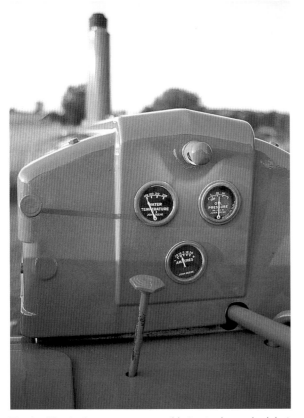

The backing in the amp gauge on this tractor is crooked, but it is good that all the gauges match in style.

Even though the steering knob on this tractor is not original, enthusiasts should not concern themselves too much with harshly criticizing people for having such things on their tractors. Farmer modifications are sometimes nice and interesting to keep on your tractors-they are a part of the machine's history.

The styled Model AR, in production from 1949 to 1953, could be fitted with engines designed specifically to burn all-fuel or gasoline. All-fuel tractors used the DLTX-72 carburetor, while gasoline units used the DLTX-71 carburetor.

One of the keys to an accurate restoration is paying special attention to paint. The owner of this tractor has apparently gone to great lengths to ensure that every nook and cranny received paint!

Later Changes

Tractor 279369 was the first fitted with many newly designed parts for the AR. The most important change was the replacement of the A3376R cylinder head with the A4226R head. Other changes included the use of a new oil pipe tappet lever.

Clutch

Deere & Company started using a new clutch adjusting disk and clutch facing disk with tractor 279500.

Powr-Trol

At serial number 279532, Deere changed the Powr-Trol idler gear and shaft. Further Powr-Trol changes, occurring at serial number 280407, involved the pump drive gear, shaft, and Woodruff key.

This view of the AR provides us with an astounding amount of information. Both tractors have the exhaust stack painted black, even though the tractor at the right has the stack at the same height as the intake stack. Furthermore, both tractors have the light bodies appropriately painted black. As for the gauge casings, one tractor has them green, while the other has them black. There is no definite answer to what color the gauge casings should be, as Deere photos show them both ways. The tractor at the right has the "JOHN DEERE" decal correctly placed on the seat backrest.

The shifter location on the Model AR had to be adjusted from its location on the row-crop models, in order to make it workable with the standard-tread design with lowered operator location.

Main Bearing Housings

At serial number 280413, Deere altered the main bearing housings of the AR as well as related components. New left- and right-hand main bearing oil pipes also appeared at this time.

Fan Shaft Ventilator Pump

The fan shaft ventilator pump and closely associated parts received alterations at serial number 280056.

Fuel System

Fuel system changes that first influenced tractor 280850 included a new fuel filter body, filter, screen, shut-off valve, and fuel cock.

Front-End Support

A new front-end "bathtub" support adorned the AR, beginning with serial number 281400, and required a change in the toolbox and the radiator tank bottom. Also necessary were a new fan shaft support and front-end baffle plate. Other

The right rear tire of the styled AR came close to the clutch pulley, but Deere knew not to get them too close together or owners would experience problems attaching belts to the pulley. During unstyled AR production, Deere made alterations to the standard placement of the rear wheels in order to afford more room between the pulley and the tire, and that was likely one thing that led to that decision.

changes included a new generator belt adjusting strap and a new belt.

Main Case and Related Parts

At serial number 282000, the A4610R main case replaced the previous A3734R main case, thus necessitating the use of a new crankcase cover, among other things. New connecting rods and bearings also were employed at this time, as were new valve tappet levers. Deere also installed a new steering worm gear.

This is what is commonly referred to as the "hood ornament" or "nose cone medallion" as found on the Model AR. Some of these Model ARs might also have had the "JOHN DEERE" 3-dimensional medallion, like the one used on the 60 installed for experimental purposes.

Paint and Decals

Like just about every other tractor in the A series, the AR and AO were primarily green tractors with yellow wheels, and all of the items that were exceptions on the row-crop and earlier standard-tread tractors were often exceptions on these tractors, as well. Unfortunately, no records have come to light that deal with changes to the decals or paint used on the styled Models AR and AO.

Production of the styled Model AR was short-lived, but the model still underwent numerous changes by production's end. This late AR bears serial number 282104 and thus is very much like the very last AR that rolled off the production line.

Serial Numbers

Serial numbers for the John Deere Model A tend to be very controversial. Various lists have been published, with some major deviations among them. The author carefully inspected most of the numbers, which are listed below as "scrapped" against the actual serial number records to help ensure that they were accurate. (Scrapped serial numbers are usually those which Deere never used on production tractors. This was often done so that major changes would occur at rounded-off or even serial numbers.) As it is possible that some errors exist or new information may come to light, the author welcomes any constructive criticism of this list.

Model A

1934	410000 to 412868		(583327 to 583999 scrapped)		(257990 to 257999 scrapped)
1935	412869 to 424024		584000 to 587348	1940	258000 to 258467
1936	424025 to 442150	1948	587349 to 611920		(258468 to 258799 scrapped)
1937	442151 to 466786	1949	611921 to 628499		258800 to 259335
1938	466787 to 476221		(628500 to 628536 scrapped)		(259336 to 259999 scrapped)
	(476222 to 476999 scrapped)		628537 to 640245	1941	260000 to 261124
1939	477000 to 478115	1950	640246 to 647069	1942	261125 to 261256
	(478116 to 478199 scrapped)		(647070 to 647999 scrapped)	1943	262157 to 262497
	478200 to 478472		648000 to 666306		(262498 to 262699 scrapped)
	(478473 to 478499 scrapped)	1951	666307 to 676746	1944	262700 to 264199
	478500 to 487249		(676747 to 676799 scrapped)		(264200 to 264299 scrapped)
	(487250 to 487360 scrapped)		676800 to 677949	1945	264300 to 265534
1940	488000 to 498535		(677950 to 677999 scrapped)	1946	265535 to 266642
	(498536 to 498558 scrapped)		678000 to 682601	1947	266643 to 268409
	498559	1952	682602 to 684380	1948	268410 to 270679
	(498560 to 498999 scrapped)		(684381 scrapped)	1949	270680 to 272984
1941	499000 to 510238		684382 to 684484	1950	272985 to 276076
1942	510239 to 520003		(684485 scrapped)	1951	276077 to 278698
1943	520004 to 522349		684486 to 685052	1952	278699 to 282349
	(522350 to 522599 scrapped)		(685053 scrapped)	1953	282350 to 284074
	522600 to 524422		685054 to 700140		
1944	524423 to 532936		(700141 to 700199 scrapped)	**Model AO-S**	
	(532937 to 532999 scrapped)		700200 to 703384	1937	1000 to 1497
	533000 to 536541		(703385 to 703999 scrapped)		(1498 to 1525 scrapped)
	(536542 to 536999 scrapped)				1526 to 1538
	537000 to 542626	**Models AR, AO**		1938	1539 to 1699
	(542647 to 542699 scrapped)	1936	250000 to 256520	1939	1700 to 1771
1945	542700 to 555333	1937	253521 to 255415		(1772 to 1799 scrapped)
1946	555334 to 569609	1938	255416 to 256699	1940	1800 to 1891
1947	569610 to 583326	1939	256700 to 257989		(1892 to 2999 scrapped)

Index